Table of Contents
Science Action Labs

1: Penny Science 5
2: Spinning Science 8
3: String Science 11
4: Body Sci-Fun 14
5: Technology: Modifying Man's Machines 18
6: Reverse Technology: Designing a Dumb Device 20
7: Brainstorming Science 21
8: A Few Great Scientists 23
9: Science, Imagination and Eggs 26
10: Science Humor 27
11: Sci-Fun 29
12: Gravity Science Fun 31
13: Problem Solving 35
14: ESP: An Unexplored Science 37
15: Möbius: A Strange Twist 39
16: Science Numbers: From Zero to Infinity 40
17: Metricopter 43
18: Can You Measure Me? 45
19: A Solar Crossword Puzzle 48
20: Science Fiction 50
21: Build a Better Boomerang 53
22: Paper Airplanes 55
23: Mirror Mirage 57
24: Charged Up with Static Electricity 59
25: Science Fables 62
Answer Key 64

Dear Teacher or Parent,

The spirit of Sir Isaac Newton will be with you and your students in this book. Newton loved science, math and experimenting. He explained the laws of gravity. He demonstrated the nature of light. He discovered how planets stay in orbit around our sun.

All the activities in this book are based upon science principles. Many are explained by Newton's laws. That is why Sir Isaac Newton has been used as a guide through the pages of this book. Newton will help your students think about, build and experiment with these activities. Newton will be with them in every activity to advise, encourage and praise their efforts.

Science Fun can help your students in many ways. Choose some activities to spice up your class demonstrations. Some **Science Fun** can be converted to hands-on lab activities for the entire class. Some can be developed into student projects or reports. Every class has a few students with a special zest for science. Encourage them to pursue some activities on their own.

Enjoy these science activities as much as Newton would have. They are designed to make your students **think**. Thinking and solving problems are what science is all about. Each **Science Fun** encourages thought. Students are often asked to come up with their best and most reasonable guess as to what will happen. Scientists call this type of guess a **hypothesis**. They are told how to assemble the materials necessary to actually try out the activities. Scientists call this **experimenting**.

Don't expect the experiments to always prove the hypothesis right. These science activities have been picked to challenge students' thinking abilities.

The answers to the activities in this book are on page 64. You will also find some science facts that will help your students understand what happened.

Here are some suggestions to help your students succeed in having Science Fun:

1. Observe carefully.
2. Follow directions.
3. Measure carefully.
4. Hypothesize intelligently.
5. Experiment safely.
6. Keep experimenting until they succeed.

Sincerely,

Ed

Edward Shevick

Name _____

Penny Science

Newton Wants You to Know

You know that it takes 100 pennies to equal a dollar. Nowadays, pennies are not worth much.

Historians think that metal coins were first made in 600 B.C. in a country that is now Turkey. Most coins are made of alloys of different metals. The pennies you will be experimenting with are made of copper and zinc.

Penny Experiments

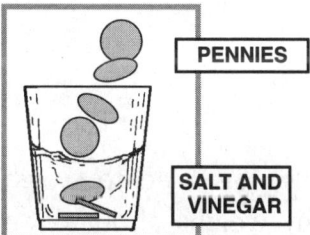

Dirty Money

Who likes dirty money? Clean your dirty pennies in a solution of salt and vinegar. Leave them in the solution for a few days.

Penny Surprise

Take a good look at a clean penny. Try to make a large drawing of all the details you see on both sides. Now here's a surprise. Use a magnifier to look at the Lincoln Memorial. You will see the image of Lincoln inside.

Penny Inertia

Your penny has inertia. This means that it doesn't want to leave you. Place a card on top of an empty glass so that part of the card sticks over the side. Place a penny in the center of the card. Use a finger to quickly flick the card beyond the glass. Your penny won't leave with the card.

5

Penny Science

Name _____

Racing Money

You are going to have a race between a quarter and a penny. Place one book on another book as shown. Roll a penny and a quarter down the book at the same time. Which coin wins the race?

Newton Hint: Look up *angular momentum* in an encyclopedia.

Glass Full of Pennies

Fill a glass to the very brim with water. Try to drop pennies **carefully** into the full glass of water. How many pennies can you drop in without any water spilling over?

Newton Hint: Look up *surface tension* in an encyclopedia.

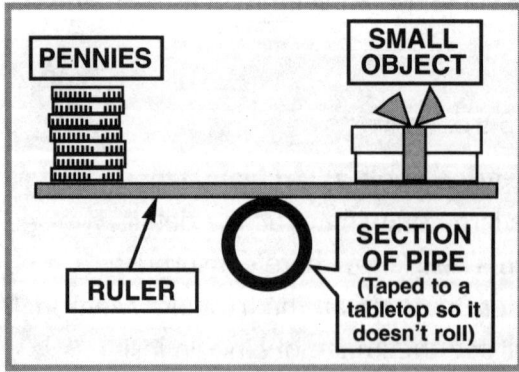

Penny Scale

A penny can also be used to weigh things. A penny weighs about three grams. There are roughly 450 grams in a pound. Construct a simple balance as shown using a ruler and a taped down section of thin pipe. Find out how many pennies (or grams) small objects weigh.

Penny Toss

What should happen if you tossed a penny and let it land 10 times? The law of averages predicts that you will get five heads and five tails. The reality is often different than the law. Try tossing your favorite penny 100 times and see if your results are average.

Penny Science

Name _____

Newton Wants You to Try More Penny Experiments

1. Find out if a penny can be attracted to a magnet.

2. Can a penny conduct heat or electricity? Use a battery (not house electricity) to check on electric conduction.

3. **How Can You Toss a Coin So It Lands on Its Edge?** It doesn't have to stay on its edge.

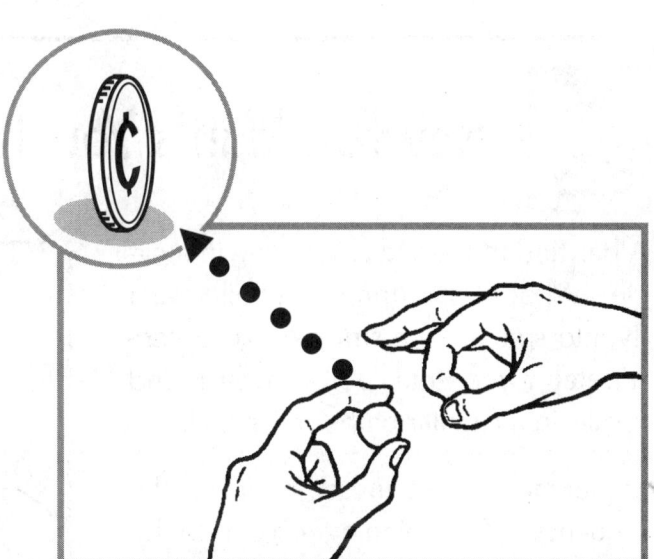

Newton Hint: Hold the coin loosely between your thumb and forefinger. Place your hand a few inches (centimeters) above a table. Snap the coin on the edge so it **spins** as it falls. Keep trying till you get it right. Try switching to quarters.

Name _____

Newton's Action Lab Science Fun 2

Spinning Science

Newton Wants You to Know

A ball tied to a string is spinning in a circle. Without the string, the ball would fly into space. The string exerts a **centripetal force** that pulls inward and results in a circular path for the ball.

Sometimes nonscientists refer to the tendency of a spinning object to be pulled outward as **centrifugal force**. That is the outward force that can separate cream from milk or remove water in your spinning clothes dryer. Hospitals use a spinning centrifuge to separate the different parts of blood.

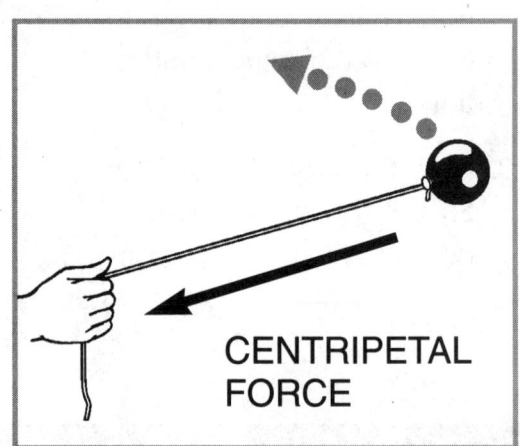

CENTRIPETAL FORCE

Spinning Experiments

Upside-Down Water Bucket

Obtain a small plastic bucket. Tie 3' (.9 m) of strong rope to the handle. Add 1" (2.5 cm) of water. **Go outside.** Carefully rotate the bucket of water vertically in a full circle. The water won't spill even when the bucket is upside down. Try spinning the bucket horizontally above your head. The water still won't spill. Can you stop the spinning without spilling the water?

8

TLC10140 Copyright © Teaching & Learning Company, Carthage, IL 62321-0010

Spinning Science

Name _____

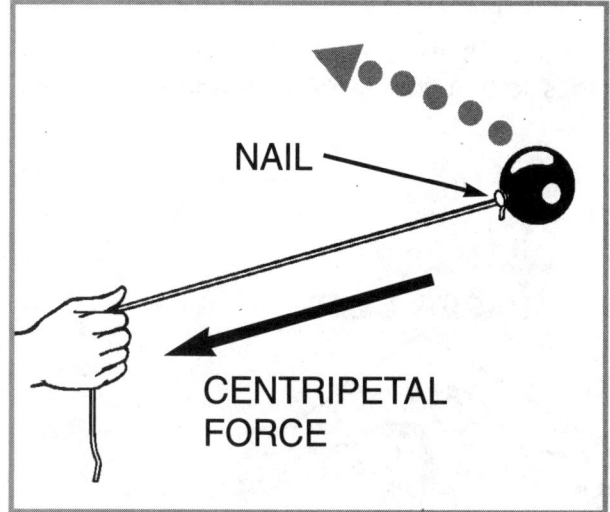

Ball into Space

Tie a nail firmly onto 3' (.9 m) of string. Shove the nail about halfway into a Styrofoam™ or other light ball. **Go outside**. Spin the string, nail and ball slowly over your head. Spin faster and faster till the ball separates from the nail. Observe the free ball's path.

You have just demonstrated the Sun-Earth relationship. Gravity represents the inward centripetal force that keeps the Earth in circular orbit. Without gravity, the Earth would shoot into space in a **straight line** just as your unattached ball did.

Spinning Force

Attach a small rubber ball to 3' (.9 m) of string. Run the string through a spool, and attach some weights to the opposite end. The combined weight of washers, nuts or "?" should be at least twice as heavy as the ball.

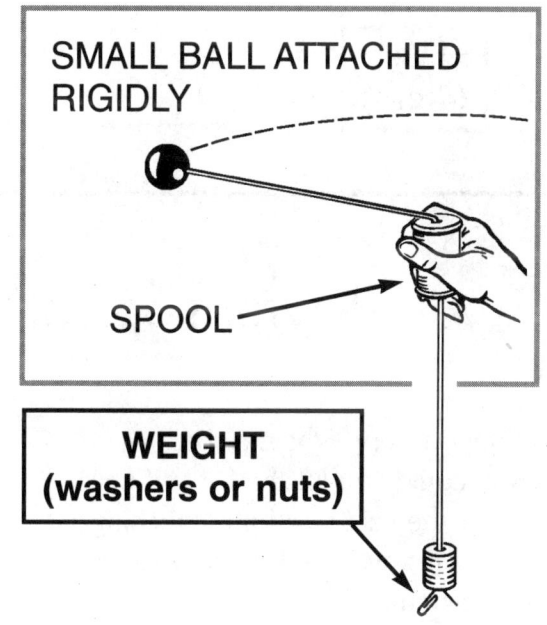

Go outside. Hold the spool firmly, and rotate the ball slowly and then rapidly. What did the heavy weight do? Stop rotating, and note how fast the ball spins as it is pulled inward. This can be related to the faster speed of the planets closest to the sun.

Building Your Own Top

Obtain a 6" or 7" (15 or 18 cm) shallow paper plate. Push a pencil through the exact center. The eraser end should stick about 1 1/2" (4 cm) beyond the **bottom** of the plate. Tape the pencil firmly to plate. Use tape on both sides of the plate.

Spinning Science

Name _____

With the eraser down, spin your paper plate top in a circle. It will surprise you how long it will spin. Try increasing the spin time by adding paper clip weights to the plate rim. Add them evenly on both sides so that your "top" is balanced.

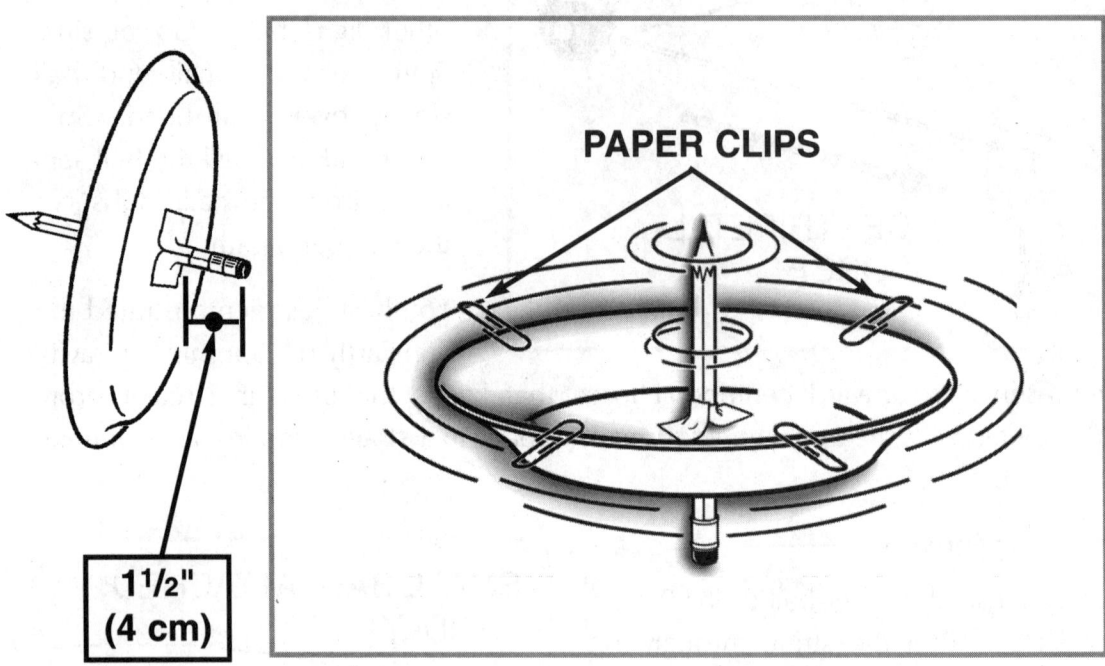

Newton's Spinning Challenge

Obtain a very light ball and a jar. How could you lift the jar and ball above the table without touching the ball in any way? Remember, this is a spinning challenge.

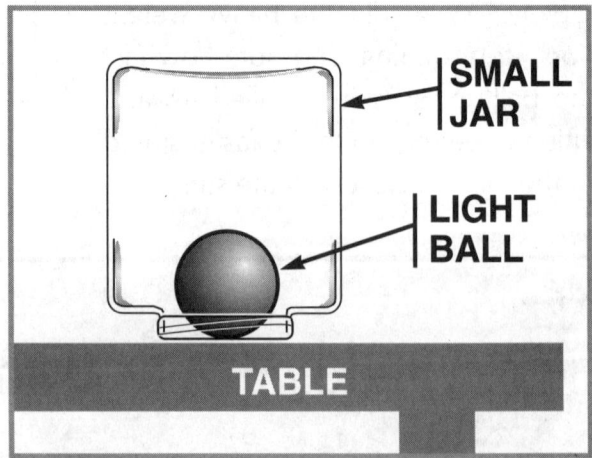

Name _____

String Science

Newton Wants You to Know

It is easy to study science with good microscopes and telescopes. It's much harder to investigate science using ordinary string. That is your job in this *Science Fun*.

String can be made from cotton, nylon or the fibers of plants called hemp or sisal. You can have thin strings like cotton thread or thick ropes like the kind that tie up ships.

String Experiments

Measuring with a String

Strings can be used to measure objects that are not straight. Simply place the string around the object being measured and line the string up with a ruler.

a. Circumference of any can is

_____ inches (centimeters).

b. Distance around your wrist is

_____ inches (centimeters).

c. Distance around your relaxed arm muscle is _____ inches (centimeters).

d. Distance around your tight arm muscle is _____ inches (centimeters).

e. Distance around your waist is _____ inches (centimeters).

Try some other string measurements.

11

String Science

Name _____

Bells from a Spoon

Cut a yard of thin string. Tie it to a metal spoon as shown. Place the string on your ears and knock the spoon against a table edge. You can get a better bell sound by having a friend knock the spoon with another spoon.

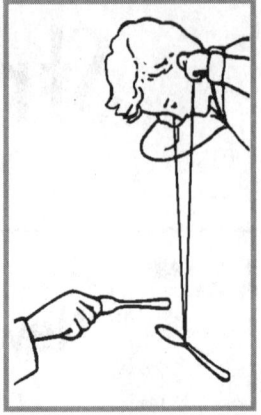

Poor Man's Fiddle

Punch a hole in a one-pound coffee can. Any similar can will do. A larger can gives better and deeper sounds.

Place about 2' (.6 m) of string through the hole, and tie a button on the inside. Tie a piece of wood (a ruler will do) at the other end of the string. Hold the can down with your foot, and use the wood to stretch the string tight. Pluck the string at various heights to "fiddle around."

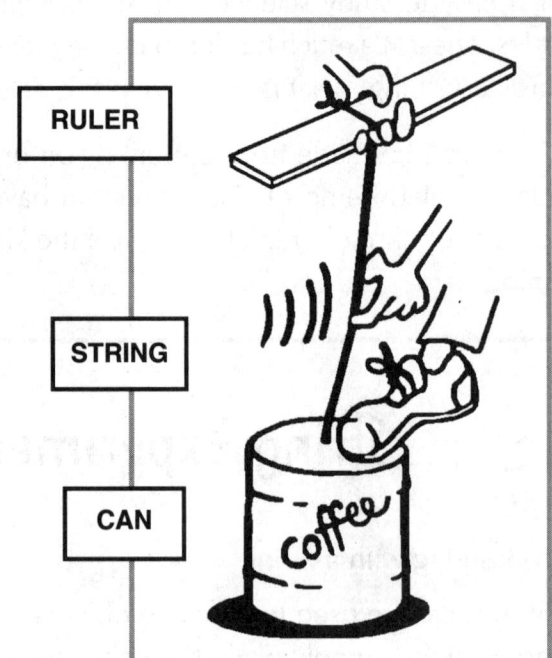

Throw Away Your Telephone

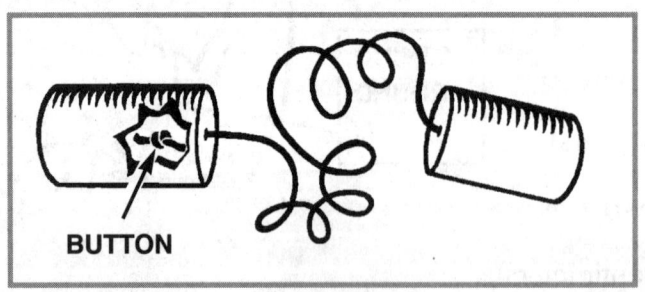

Obtain two similar empty juice or soda cans. Use a can opener to remove the drinking end. Punch a nail hole through the opposite end. Obtain about 50' (15 m) of string. Place the string ends through the holes and tie each end to a button. Pull the strings tight and take turns talking or listening to a friend.

To improve your tin can phone, try different strings, cans or wax the strings.

Newton's Favorite Waterfall

Have you ever observed water falling from a faucet? The falling water forms a tube instead of scattering. The falling water is held by a characteristic called **surface tension**. Surface tension is due to water molecules attracting each other to form a water skin.

You can use water's surface tension plus some string to make Newton's waterfall.

1. Obtain an 8" (20 cm) section of string. If the string is too thick, braid four sections into a thicker string.

2. Obtain a **small** container with a pouring spout. You can use a beaker, measuring cup, graduate or a small pitcher.

3. Hold the string firmly with your finger at the **back** of the pitcher.

4. Hold the other end of the string against the **inside** of a glass.

5. Hold the glass just below the pouring container and carefully pour the water along the string. It will form a tube around the string.

6. As you pour, you can move the glass further away. Your waterfall will still work.

Body Sci-Fun

Newton's Eye Exam

Newton loves optical illusions. Which of the two **inner** circles is the largest? _____

1. Measure the diameter of both a and b's inner circles. What did you discover? _____

   _____

   _____

a.

b.

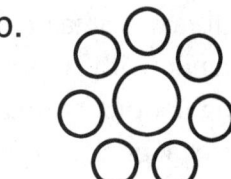

Your next eye test involves **peripheral vision**. Peripheral vision allows humans to observe the world from both sides as well as in front. Your eyes can rotate within their bony sockets. Your entire head can swivel.

Even when both head and eyes are kept straight ahead. You can still see quite a bit on both sides. This activity will check your ability to see at the periphery (outer edges) of your vision. A person with poor peripheral vision will have difficulty with driving, sports and work.

2. Obtain two yardsticks and a deck of cards.

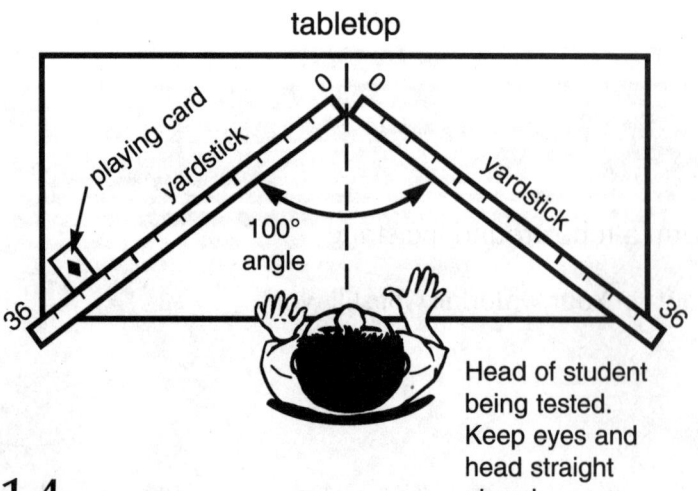

3. Set the yardsticks up as shown.

4. Have the student being tested place his or her **chin** on the table. The student should stare ahead and try not to move his or her eyes or head.

5. Pick a card at random. Face it toward the student. Move it slowly forward from the 36" (91 cm) position until the student can identify the card.

6. Try both the left and right sides using different cards.

Body Sci-Fun

Name _____

At what inch (centimeter) did the right eye identify the card? _____

At what inch (centimeter) did the left eye identify the card? _____

7. Try the peripheral vision test on other students.

Newton's Heaviness Experiment

You've learned that your eyes can easily be fooled by illusions. So can your muscles.

1. Obtain two cans with lids.

2. Fill one completely with sand or dirt. Seal and tape the lid. Mark it *H* for "heavy."

3. Fill the second can one-fourth full of sand or dirt. Seal and tape the lid. Mark it *L* for "light."

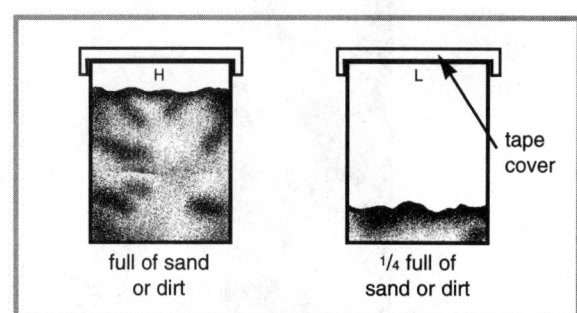

full of sand or dirt   ¼ full of sand or dirt   tape cover

4. Blindfold a student and place him or her standing at a table with the two cans. Place one hand above, but not touching, the heavy can.

5. Guide the student to pick up the heavy can on your signal. The student is to pick up the can and vigorously raise it high. Then the student should place the can back on the table and await your next signal. Have this done five to eight times.

6. Sometime during this sequence, secretly switch to the light can.

What happened to the student's arm when you switched to the lighter can? _____
_____

7. Repeat, starting with the light can and switching to the heavy can. What happened this time? _____

8. Repeat, using other students.

Bet You Can't Pick Me Up

All objects have a center of gravity. This is the point where things are balanced. Your body also has a center of gravity. You can't do certain simple tasks when you are out of balance.

15

TLC10140 Copyright © Teaching & Learning Company, Carthage, IL 62321-0010

Body Sci-Fun

Name _____

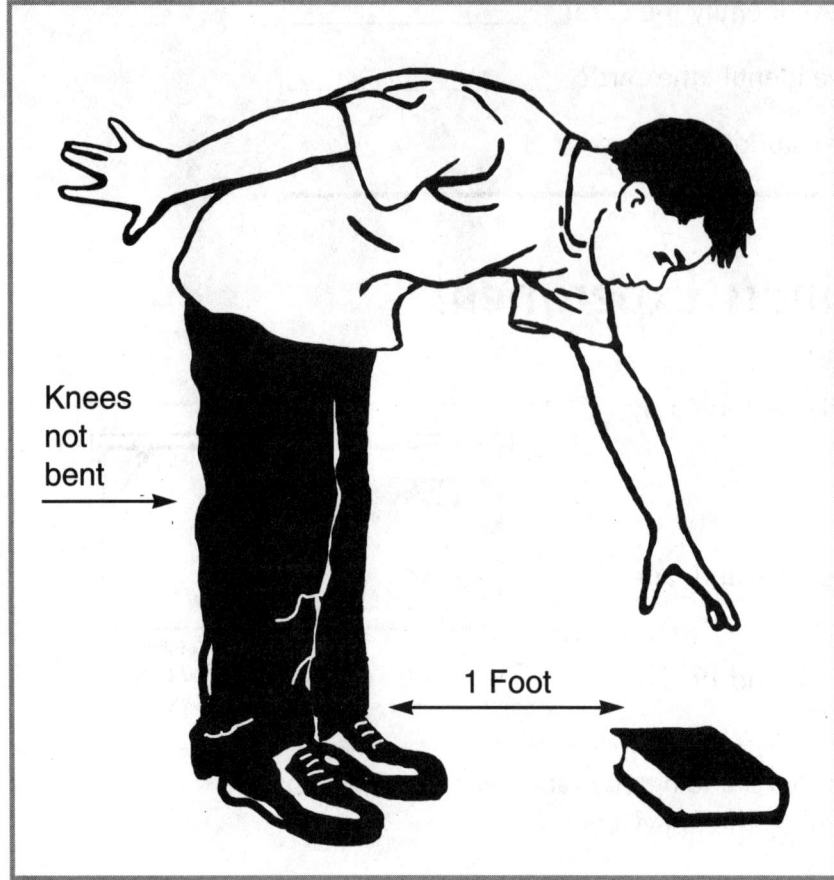

Knees not bent →

1 Foot

1. Obtain a light textbook.
2. Have a boy stand 1' (.3 m) away from the textbook.
3. Have the boy try to lean over and pick up the textbook. The boy can lean over but should **not bend his knees**.

What were the results of this bending experiment? _____
_____
_____
_____
_____
_____
_____

Try the experiment on other boys.

What were the results for most boys? _____
_____
_____
_____

4. Notice you have used boys in this experiment. Now try the same experiment with girls.

What were your results with girls? _____
_____
_____
_____

If you found any differences, the answer is that body weight is distributed differently for boys and girls.

Body Sci-Fun

Name _____

Body Words

There are four body words on each line. Can you find the word which **least** belongs with the rest?

Example: hinged, **bronchi**, gliding, fixed

Bronchi is part of the lungs. The other words describe body joints.

1. Molar, Incisor, Villi, Canine

2. Artery, Vein, Capillary, Plasma

3. Atrium, Pepsin, Rennin, Gastric Juice

4. Bronchi, Alveoli, Trachea, Rectum

5. Pylorus, Cartilage, Ligament, Tendon

6. Liver, Pancreas, Esophagus, Bile

7. Plasma, White Blood Cells, Red Blood Cells, Vein

8. Cartilage, Muscle, Biceps, Triceps

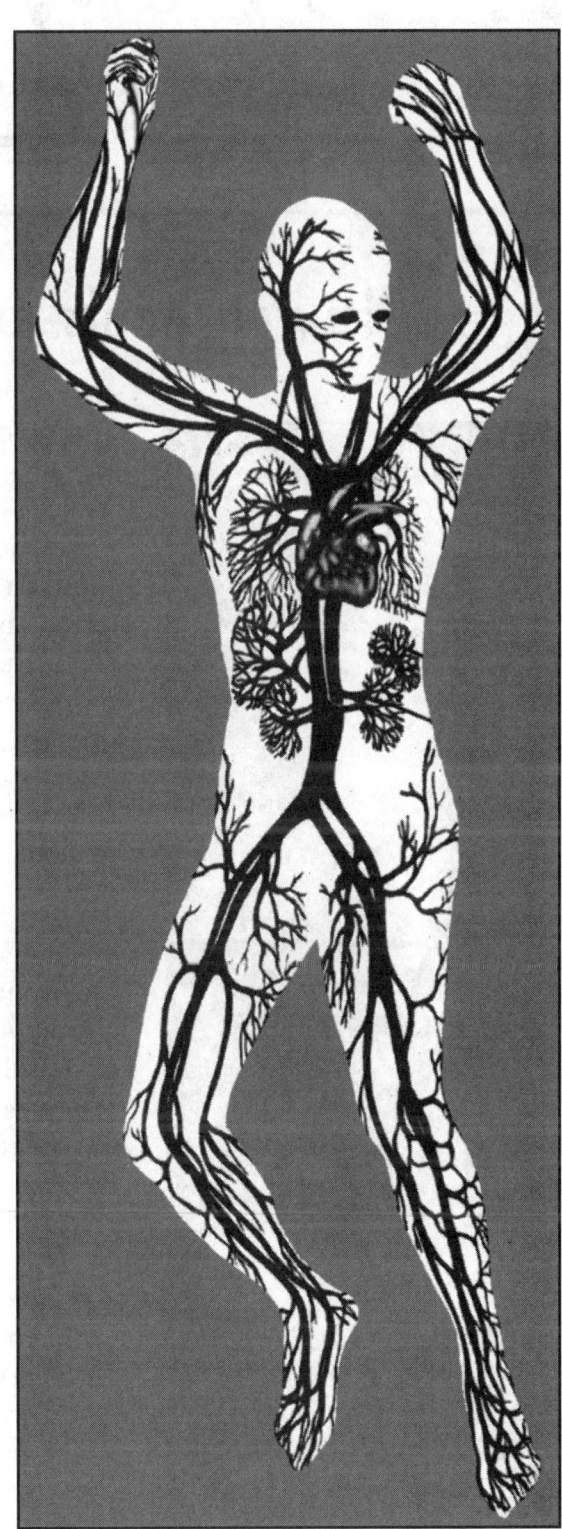

17

Newton's Action Lab Science Fun 5

Name _____

Technology: Modifying Man's Machines

Newton Wants You to Know

Technology enables man to supply his needs by the use of tools and machinery instead of by muscles and sweat. Scientists discover new ideas and technologists, such as engineers, apply their discoveries in building better products. The laser was developed by scientists doing "pure" research. Lasers are now used for drilling diamonds, attaching eye retinas and aligning bridges. The transistor came out of research on "solid state" physics and has enabled engineers to construct radios and computers the size of matchboxes.

Technology can supply us with cheaper and better items from staplers to cameras. It can also create many of man's problems. Automobiles solve personal transportation problems but congest and pollute our cities. Early man invented the bow and arrow to be able to kill his enemies at greater distances. Modern technology enables us to launch a nuclear missile 7000 miles (11,270 km) to its target.

Technology has both great promises and great problems. This activity will ask you to concentrate on the promises by designing, building and modifying some technological devices.

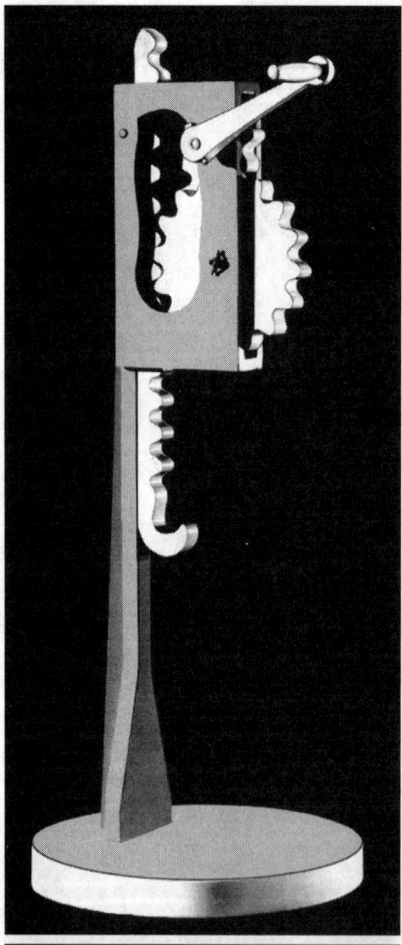

Da Vinci's model of a jack to lift heavy objects

Technology: Modifying Man's Machines

Name _____

Technology Tasks

Try to design and build devices in the following four categories:

Applying Common Devices to New Tasks

Take an everyday product or device and use it in a different way. Blow through a straw to cool things off. Use a paper clip as a laboratory weight. Use a mousetrap to protect your property from your little brother.

Modifying a Common Device

Take a common device and **change** it or **add** to it to make it do a new job. Attach razor blades to a rake so it cuts grass as well as rakes up the clippings. Place rubber on nail heads so they make less noise when pounded.

Replacing Common Devices

Find a better way to do a job now done by a tool or gadget. Use a steel glove to replace a hammer. Develop a new lubricant that reduces friction so much that wheels become obsolete. Use a blast of air to replace scissors in cutting material.

Inventing New Devices

Uncover some current need of man. Apply your vast technological skills to solving it. Man could use a smog mask, teaching devices, cheaper home building materials or "?".

Newton Wants You to Improve the Human Machine

Build a device which will enable us to make better use of our five senses. Find ways to compensate for such defects as deafness, blindness or being crippled. You can invent a new and simpler Braille, attach a device to the ear to improve hearing or design a better artificial limb or heart.

Now make yourself rich. Go beyond a design and actually build a model of your great technology.

NEWTON'S ACTION LAB

Science Fun 6

Name _____

Reverse Technology: Designing a Dumb Device

Newton Wants You to Know

Scientists and engineers make a living designing new and useful products. This Newton activity encourages you to **reverse** technology. Your challenge is to design a series of devices with such obvious faults that no one would dare use them.

Any great engineer can design useful products. It takes a genius like you to reverse technology and design something stupid.

Technology Follies

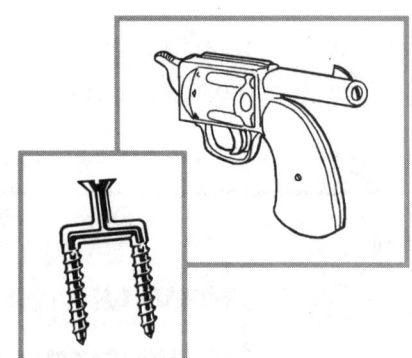

1. Don't fire this gun. It is not the smartest design in the world.
2. Don't try to turn these screws.

Newton's Reverse Technology Challenge

Try to come up with stupid designs in these three areas:

1. Design a stupid household product.
2. Design an automobile aid.
3. Free spirit design: Do your dumb design in any area of your choice.

20

TLC10140 Copyright © Teaching & Learning Company, Carthage, IL 62321-0010

Name _____

Brainstorming Science

 Newton Wants You to Know

Scientists try to think differently than most people. They solve some problems by trial and error. They solve other problems by patient, hard work. There are many ways to solve scientific problems.

Sometimes the solution to a problem comes from an off-beat method called **brainstorming**. Brainstorming involves coming up with imaginative, wild and improbable ideas. In brainstorming, two times two is not always four. No solution is ruled out even if at first it seems off-the-wall or lunatic.

Brainstorming doesn't require a laboratory, supplies or equipment. All you need is a fertile mind that looks at things differently.

 Brainstorming Bricks

Help! Your dad's factory in Azuza makes regular red and gray building bricks. Your dad made over a million bricks for an order that has been cancelled. No one wants these bricks to build walls.

Brainstorming time. Forget bricks are for building. Can you come up with at least four imaginative and different uses for bricks?

1. _____   2. _____

3. _____   4. _____

TLC10140 Copyright © Teaching & Learning Company, Carthage, IL 62321-0010

21

Brainstorming Science

Name _____

More Brainstorming Problems

You Are Getting Smaller

Some genius at Harvard University discovered a fluid with a remarkable property. A few drops placed on **anything** you can imagine becomes 10 times smaller. Brainstorm four great ways to use the fluid.

1. _____   2. _____

3. _____   4. _____

Good-Bye Gravity

Not to be outdone by magic fluids, scientists at Cal Tech have discovered a powder that eliminates gravity. How would you use it?

1. _____   2. _____

3. _____   4. _____

Newton's Peacetime Brainstorm

During the Cold War years between the United States and Russia, both sides dug hundreds of huge underground silos. The silos were used to store and hide nuclear missiles.

Now the U.S. is friendlier with Russia. Both countries are destroying their missiles. Both are stuck with hundreds of huge holes in the ground.

Newton wants you to brainstorm four great ideas for using these silos for peaceful purposes.

1. _____   2. _____

3. _____   4. _____

Name _____

A Few Great Scientists

NEWTON'S ACTION LAB
Science Fun
8

Andreas Vesalius

Vesalius' Sketch of Human Muscles

Vesalius was born in Belgium in 1514. He grew up to become physician to the Roman Emperor.

During his medical studies, he began to have doubts about his professor's knowledge of the human body. He and all the other medical students were being taught false ideas about the structure of the human body.

After years of study, Vesalius published a book on anatomy (body structure). His drawings of muscles and bones were both beautiful and accurate. Today's physicians are all indebted to Vesalius.

Edward Jenner

Edward Jenner was born in England in 1749. At that time people all over Europe were dying from a disease called smallpox. Smallpox killed almost 10% of the population.

Jenner observed that milkmaids almost never died of smallpox. Instead they got a minor disease called cowpox. Cowpox gave the milkmaids sores but was never fatal.

TLC10140 Copyright © Teaching & Learning Company, Carthage, IL 62321-0010

A Few Great Scientists

Name _____

Jenner had a theory. Perhaps cowpox prevented smallpox. He tested his theory by infecting a young boy with cowpox. Six weeks later he placed a small cut on the boy's arm and infected him with the real smallpox. The boy stayed healthy.

What Jenner did is now called vaccination. Thanks to his work, you can now be vaccinated against the flu, polio and many other diseases.

Marie Sklodowska Curie

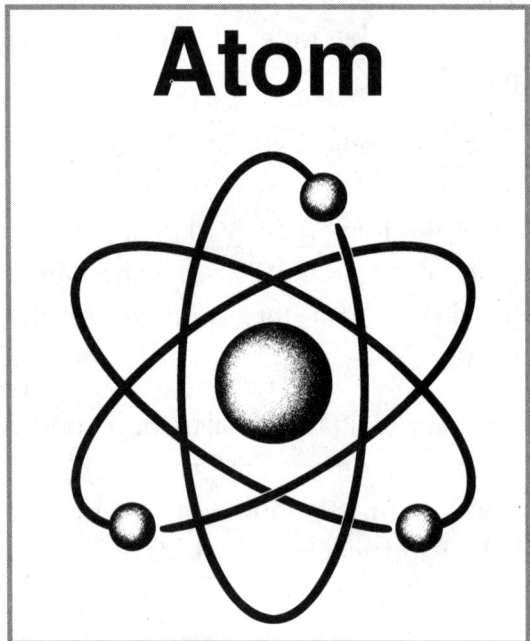

Marie Curie was born in Poland in 1867. She went to France to study physics and chemistry. She married a physics professor and both began the study of natural radioactivity given off by rocks.

They discovered the atoms called radium and polonium. Notice that polonium was named after her native Poland. She and her husband shared the 1903 Nobel Prize in physics.

Marie Curie founded the Radium Institute in Paris. She spent her life discovering ways to use radium as a health tool.

Albert Einstein

Albert Einstein was born in Germany in 1879. Little Albert showed no early signs of being a genius. He didn't talk until age three. At five, his father gave him a pocket compass. Albert marveled at how it always pointed in the same direction.

A Few Great Scientists

Name _____

During high school Albert rebelled against being "forced" to learn. He wanted to educate himself at his own speed and in his own way. He dropped out of one school. He failed the entrance exams to college. It took Albert an additional year studying high school biology before he was finally admitted to college.

Albert rebelled again in college and disturbed his professors. One called him a "lazy dog." He disliked laboratory work and preferred to work problems out in his head. Fellow students helped him cram for exams so he could finally graduate.

Einstein's great scientific and mathematical mind opened new frontiers about matter, energy, light and gravity. His famous formula $E = MC^2$ equated energy and matter. From his work came both the nuclear bomb and nuclear energy.

Newton Wants You to Research a Special Scientist

Scientists and their discoveries make interesting reading. Pick one of the great scientists below and learn as much as you can about him or her.

Aristotle	Drew	Lister
Audubon	Edison	Marconi
Bohr	Fahrenheit	Mead
Burbank	Franklin	Newton
Carver	Fermi	Pasteur
Da Vinci	Galileo	Pavlov
Darwin	Harvey	Urey

Name _____

Science, Imagination and Eggs

Newton Wants You to Know

Besides being curious and asking questions, a scientist must also have a good **imagination**. People with good imaginations can create pictures in their minds that help solve problems.

Use your imagination on some egg problems. Feel free to come up with wild, strange and humorous answers. Turn your imagination loose.

"Egg"magination

Colored Eggs

Most eggs are white or brown. Why should they come only in those two colors? Imagine a color code for eggs that could be useful to people.

New Egg Shape

Eggs are oval. That's a great shape. Can you imagine some better shapes for eggs?

New Eggshell

Eggshells break easily. Your imagination is in control. What should eggshells be made of so they don't break easily?

Bigger and Better Eggs

Assume the world is stuck with chickens that lay white or brown, oval, thin-shelled eggs. What could you do to chickens to encourage them to produce bigger and better eggs?

Eggs from the Sky

A mysterious egg from a distant planet fell out of the sky and landed in your backyard. What might the egg hatch into?

Newton Wants You to Imagine More

Man is puzzled by the problem of getting rid of all the garbage he creates. Since eggshells are normally thrown away, they contribute to the garbage problems. Imagine some new uses for eggshells so that people will want to save them.

Name _____

Science Humor

Newton Wants You to Know

Besides being extra bright, most scientists have a sharp sense of humor. Good scientists are also warm human beings. They enjoy science and working with their fellow scientists.

Take the science students at Cal Tech (California Institute of Technology) in Pasadena, California. These young people are among the top 1% of the brains of their generation. Yet no one can describe them as humorless grinds who do nothing but spout mathematical formulas all day. Some of the greatest college practical jokes have been perpetrated by Cal Tech students. These range from breaking down a full size car and reassembling it on the gym roof to flying saucer hoaxes.

Newton wants you to practice your skills in scientific humor. Maybe Cal Tech will hear of you!

Humor Practice

You Mean the World Isn't Round?

Everyone today knows that the Earth is round. Back in the days of Columbus, most people were sure that the Earth was flat. It seemed logical because the Earth appears flat. They were certain that a ship that ventured too far would fall over the Earth's edge.

Newton wants you to prove that the Earth is really flat. Come up with some seemingly "logical" arguments for a flat Earth. Challenge some of your "normal" friends to a debate on the subject. You don't have to be right. Use humor to demolish their round-Earth arguments.

TLC10140 Copyright © Teaching & Learning Company, Carthage, IL 62321-0010

Science Humor

Name _____

Reincarnation

People who believe in reincarnation think that they have lived before in a different time and place. Humor them. Invent a story about your own reincarnation. You can be anyone in anytime period you wish. Enjoy.

It's the Law

Newton and Galileo gave us many laws about the natural world we live in. They both worked on laws explaining the motions of planets, stars and falling bodies. Join Newton and Galileo by proposing a **pseudolaw** (false law) and defending it. For example, your **pseudolaw** could prove that snowflakes fall because white objects are attracted to the Earth. You don't have to be right. Just be humorous.

Newton Wants to Live Forever

Help Newton live longer. Conjure up a device, fluid or power source that can increase a person's life span. Write a radio or TV commercial to sell your fake product. Go into unscientific and semi-scientific details to convince people to buy your longer life idea. Have fun! This is a humor project.

Name _____

Sci-Fun

Newton Wants You to Enjoy Science

Newton is proud of you. You've learned more science at your age than Newton ever knew at the same age. This section is for you to relax and enjoy.

Sci-Fun

Two-Faced Illusion

Optical illusions try to fool you with lines, shapes or colors. Observe the classic optical illusion on the right. Keep looking until you see a pretty face and the face of a witch.

AN OPTICAL ILLUSION

Can you see two faces?

Dancing Cup

Obtain two paper cups. Place one cup **loosely** inside the other. Blow through a straw at the space between the cups. Observe the dance of the cup.

Newton would make a big deal of this activity. He would compare what you did to boats and trains that lift themselves above a surface using air pressure.

Out of Balance

Tape a ruler and a hammer together as shown. Try balancing it as shown at the edge of a table. You may have to adjust the ruler, hammer or tape.

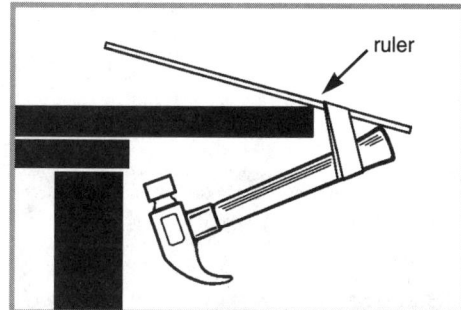

Sci-Fun

Name _____

Rocket Fun

Obtain a plastic squeeze bottle. Find a straw, and cut a 3½" (8.9 cm) section. Fold the straw over at one end, as shown, and tape it so that it is air-tight.

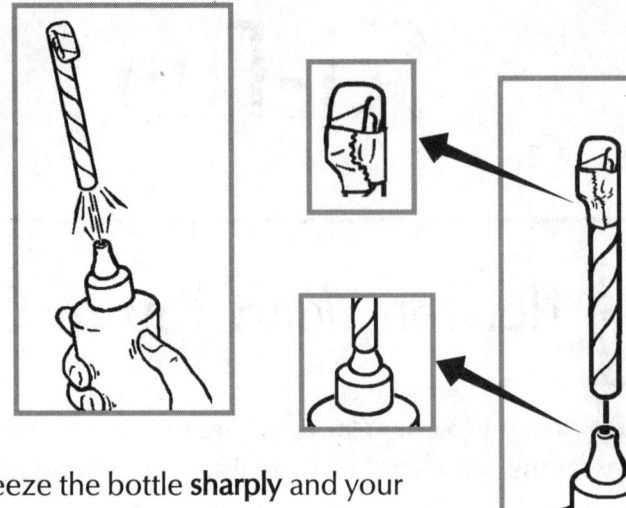

Place the open end of the straw on the nozzle of the squeeze bottle. Squeeze the bottle **sharply** and your straw rockets into space.

Newton wants to claim this as part of his Action-Reaction Theory. What do you think?

Newton's Magic Can Design

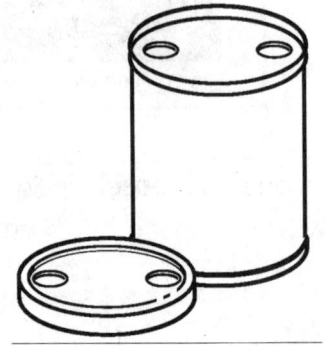

Newton likes to be obeyed. That's why he designed this can that always rolls back to him.

Obtain a coffee or nut can with a lid. Punch two nail holes in the can bottom and the lid as shown.

Obtain a long strong rubber band. Cut it so that it is one long piece.

Obtain a fishing weight or some heavy nuts.

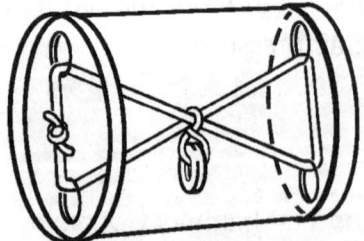

String the rubber band through the ends and through the weight as shown. Tie the rubber band ends.

Roll the can away from you. It should come back to you.

Newton Note: You are storing energy in the rubber band as you roll the can away from you.

Name _____

Gravity Sci-Fun

Newton Explains Center of Gravity

Every object has a center of gravity. That is the point where all its mass (similar to weight) is evenly distributed.

Your body has a center of gravity. If you bend too far forward or backward, you will fall.

Cars are built low to have a low center of gravity. Imagine making a sharp turn in a 20' (6 m) high car. The high car would have its center of gravity shifted and fall over.

You've seen a picture of the famous leaning Tower of Pisa in Italy. It is 180' (54 m) high. It leans to one side almost 15' (4.5 m). If it leans to the side a bit more, it would topple because its center of gravity has changed.

Scientists are now working on plans to keep the leaning tower from falling. What would you suggest that they do?

The Leaning Tower of Pisa

180 Feet Tall
15 Foot Tilt

_____
_____
_____
_____
_____

Gravity Sci-Fun

Name _____

Fun with Center of Gravity

Here are a few ways to demonstrate center of gravity. Observe the weighted horse. It looks like it should fall off the table. It doesn't because the attached weight moves its center of gravity directly under its rear legs.

Study the center of gravity setups below. Try to build as many as you can.

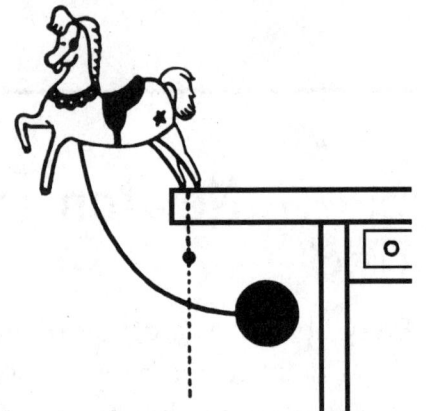

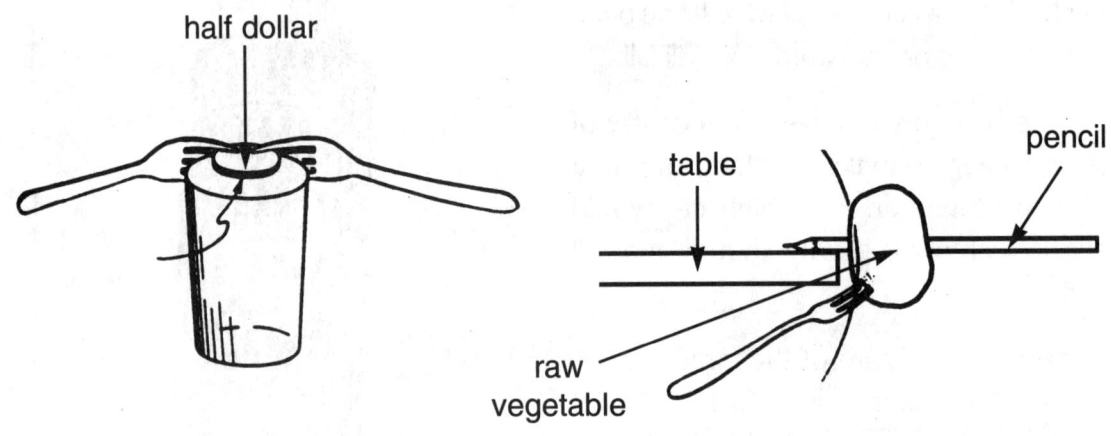

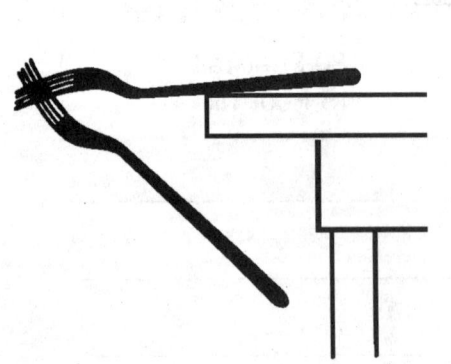

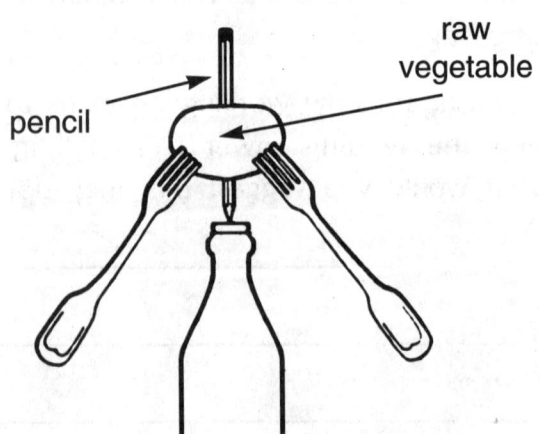

32

TLC10140 Copyright © Teaching & Learning Company, Carthage, IL 62321-0010

Gravity Sci-Fun

Name _____

Airplane Balance

This airplane demonstrates center of balance.

1. Cut out a piece of cardboard this shape. 5" x 8" (13 x 20 cm) file cards work fine.
2. Tape a penny on both sides under the rear elevator as shown.
3. Now try to balance your plane placing your finger **under** the point shown.
4. Color and decorate your balancing plane to make the airlines envious.

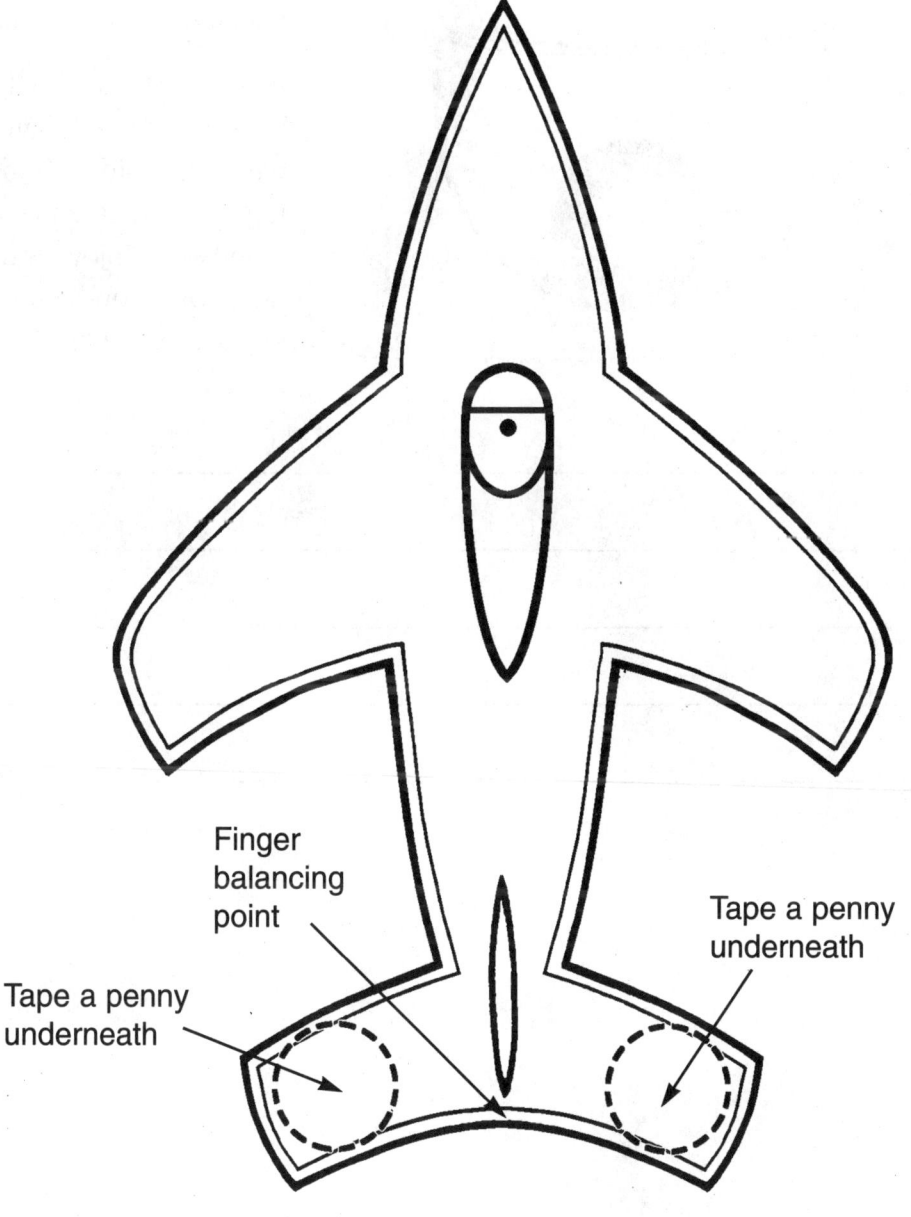

Gravity Sci-Fun

Name _____

An Unbalanced Egg

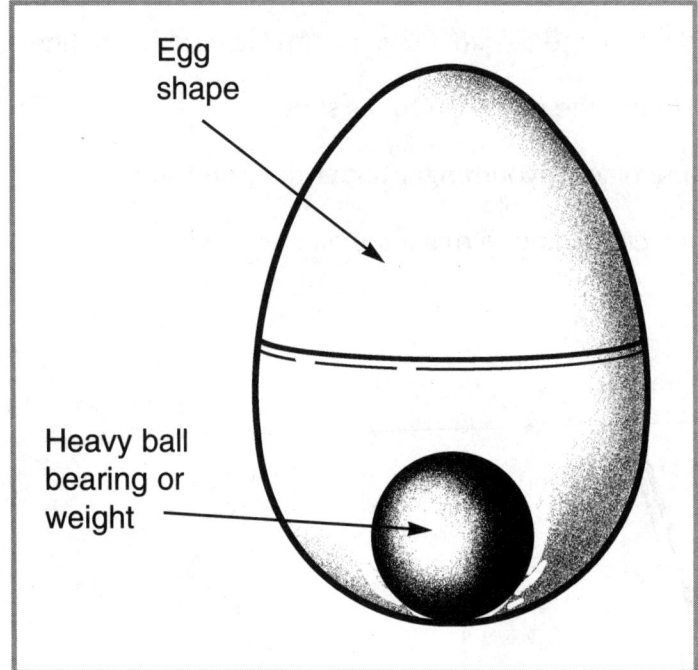

Here is a gravity toy that you can build. It can be used to amaze your friends.

1. Obtain a plastic egg. This can be a leftover Easter decoration or the type that hosiery is sold in.

2. Place a heavy ball bearing (or a heavy weight) inside, and tape the two halves together. Enjoy and describe how your egg acts as you push it around.

_____
_____
_____
_____
_____

Name _____

Problem Solving

Newton Wants You to Know

The basic job of a scientist is problem solving. Some problems can be solved by trial and error. Some need math for their solution. Scientists have their own way of solving problems.

Thomas Alva Edison solved many problems while working on his thousand plus inventions. His incandescent light bulb invention required solving at least two problems. Edison used trial and error to find a filament that would burn a long time. Then he enclosed his filament in a glass bulb and pumped out the air. This solved his other problem of keeping the air from burning up the filament.

Problem Solving with Math

Frog in the Well Problem

A frog was at the bottom of a 30' (9 m) well. He wanted to see the world. Each day he climbed up 5' (4.5 m) but slid back 4' (1.2 m). How many days did it take our poor tired frog to escape the well? _____

Mixed-Up Socks Problem

You have 10 red socks and 10 blue socks in a drawer. Except for color, all 20 socks are the same. If you had your *eyes closed*, how many socks must you take out of the drawer to be sure you have a matched pair? _____

Problem Solving

Name _____

House and Lot Problem

You bought a house and a lot for $50,000.00. The house costs $40,000 more than the lot. How much did the lot cost? _____

Poison Pill Problem

A pharmacist placed 12 similar tablets in a bottle. They all looked exactly alike. However, one was a poisonous pill that differed from the other 11 by being heavier.

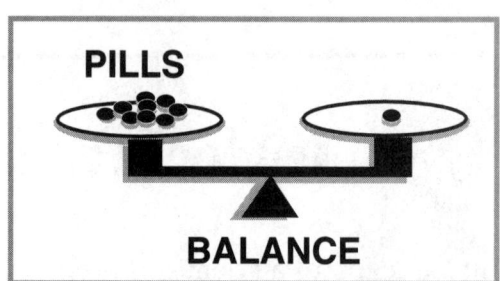

The pharmacist solved his problem by weighing the pills on his balance. It took him only three weighings to find the poison pill. How do you think he found it? _____

Problem Solving by Manual Manipulation

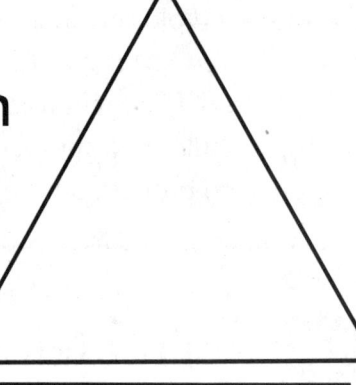

Trace the triangle on the right on a piece of cardboard. Make four exact copies and cut them out. Can you assemble the four small triangles to make one large triangle?

Newton's Favorite Gravity Problem

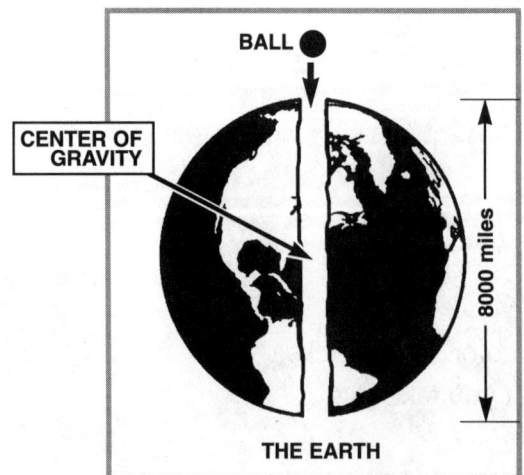

An imaginary hole 3' (.9 m) in diameter is drilled 8000 miles (12,880 km) completely through the Earth. A ball is dropped through the hole.

Can you describe in detail the path that the ball will take?

Newton wants to help. Assume that the ball does not melt due to the Earth's heat. Assume for scientific purposes that the Earth's center of gravity is 4000 miles (6440 km) down.

Name _____

ESP: An Unexplored Science

NEWTON'S ACTION LAB
Science Fun
14

Newton Wants You to Know

ESP is an abbreviation for Extra Sensory Perception. It involves abilities above and beyond the normal human senses. ESP challenges many of the accepted laws of science. Scientists are not sure there is such a thing as ESP Yet more and more scientists are doing ESP research. They feel that science should be open to new ideas and are willing to set up controlled experiments to determine the truth.

Three of the most common forms of ESP are defined below. You will need to understand these definitions if you are to experiment with them scientifically.

1. **TELEPATHY:** Communication from one person to another without the use of the ordinary five senses. **Example:** A person could reproduce a drawing of a shape sent to him by a "sender" from a distant city.

2. **PSYCHOKINESIS:** Control of objects by the influence of the mind. Sometimes this is called "mind over matter." **Example:** A nail could be bent or a tossed coin could be influenced to land heads up.

3. **CLAIRVOYANCE:** Awareness of an event or object without the use of the ordinary five senses. **Example:** A clairvoyant person could locate a lost child or tell you what's inside a sealed envelope.

Telepathy Experiment

Start out by reviewing the definition of *telepathy*. Find a deck of cards and pick out the *ace* through *five* of the spades and hearts. You'll end up with 10 cards. Shuffle them.

Find a friend who may share your telepathic power. Stare at the deck, one card at a time, and mentally send the image to your friend. The friend should be informed that you are sending five spades and five hearts. Let the friend write the numbers *1* to *10* and identify each card as you "send" it. Getting three out of 10 right would be great telepathy. Try other friends, or have them "send" to you.

37

ESP: An Unexplored Science

Name _____

Psychokinesis Experiment

Review the definition of *psychokinesis*. Obtain a pair of dice. You'll only need one for this experiment.

Write *one* to *10* on a piece of paper. Concentrate on any one number from *one* to *six*. Use PK (psychokinetic) powers to "control" the die.

Roll the die and see if it "obeyed" your command. Try 10 rolls. Getting three out of 10 right would be great PK.

Experiment with friends. Try to find someone with PK power.

Clairvoyance Experiment

Review the definition of *clairvoyance*. Pick the ace to 10 of spades out of a deck of cards. Shuffle the 10 spades, and place them facedown on a table. Mark *one* to *10* on paper and try to "see" through each card. Write what you think they are. Three out of 10 right would be great clairvoyance.

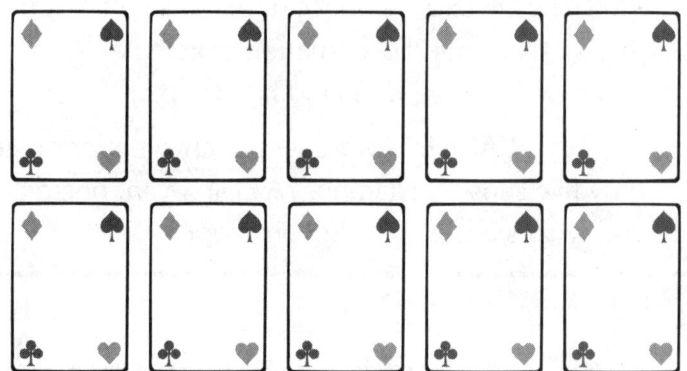

Newton Wants You to Explore ESP Further

There are many variations on ESP You could blindfold someone and hand him or her playing cards. Could he or she identify red or black?

Maybe you could send telepathic messages better if you had more than one person doing the sending. Are adults better at ESP than young people?

Name _____

Möbius: A Strange Twist

Newton Wants You to Know

Newton owes this experiment to August Ferdinand Möbius (1790-1868). He was a German astronomer and mathematician who helped discover a science called **topology**. Topology is useful in interpreting heights on maps.

Constructing a Möbius Strip

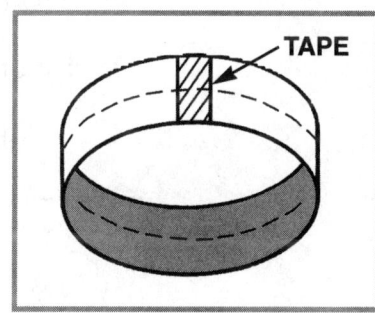

Simple Strip

Cut a 2" (5 cm) strip along the length of a piece of notebook paper. Overlap the edges about 1" (2.5 cm) to form a paper circle. Tape the edges.

Cut down the center of the circle (as shown by the dotted lines) to obtain two smaller paper circles.

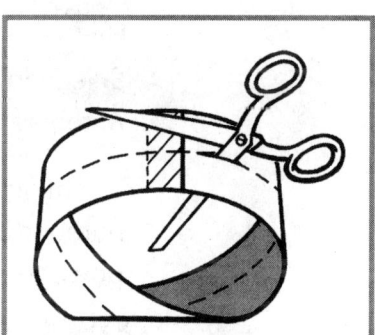

Real Möbius Strip

Again cut a 2" (5 cm) strip along the length of notebook paper. This time, give the paper a half twist (180°) before taping the 1" (2.5 cm) overlap together.

Cut down the center of your Möbius strip, and you are in for a surprise.

Newton Wants You to Go Further

Write a message on the paper strip before making another Möbius strip.

Cut a completed Möbius strip down the center again. Is your message on the inside or outside of your strip?

39

Name _____

Science Numbers: From Zero to Infinity

Newton Loves Numbers

Science and math cannot be separated. A physicist explains matter and motion in math terms. An astronomer deals with huge numbers. Here are some larger and small numbers scientists deal with constantly.

1. Distance from the Earth to the sun . . . . 100,000,000 kilometers
2. Height of Mount Everest . . . . 10,000 meters
3. Size of a typical flea . . . . $1/1000$ of a meter
4. Size of a disease virus . . . . $1/10,000,000$ of a meter

Scientific Notation

Scientific notation is a method scientists use to handle very small and very large numbers. Learning it will not be easy. Your best brain cells will be challenged.

Scientific notation is based upon the fact that any number can be first written as a number between one and 10. This number is followed by a **power** of 10. The power of 10 keeps track of the zeros you need.

Examples

$5000 = 5 \times 1000 = 5 \times 10^3$ ← (power of 10)
$500 = 5 \times 100 = 5 \times 10^2$
$50 = 5 \times 10 = 5 \times 10^1$
$5 = 5 \times 1 = 5 \times 10^0$ ← (10^0 means **no** zero)
$0.5 = 5 \times .1 = 5 \times 10^{-1}$
$0.05 = 5 \times .01 = 5 \times 10^{-2}$
$0.005 = 5 \times .001 = 5 \times 10^{-3}$

Science Numbers: From Zero to Infinity

Name _____

Notice that each example ends up as a number between one and 10 and some power of 10. The power is sometimes called an exponent. It keeps track of the decimal point.

Now for some practice problems. Remember to change the numbers given to a number between one and 10 plus a power of 10.

Review Examples:

$350 = 3.5 \times 100 = 3.5 \times 10^2$

$0.56 = 5.6 \times 10^{-1}$

1. 3700

2. 25,000

3. 400,000

4. 2,800,000

5. 0.2

6. 0.005

7. 0.0018

8. 0.00007

Newton Wants You to Enjoy Numbers

Here are some interesting time and distance measurements. Just enjoy them. If you feel ambitious, try converting them to scientific notation.

Age of the Earth	over 5,000,000,000 years
Time since dinosaur age	60,000,000 years
Radius of the Earth	10,000,000 meters
Earth to moon distance	100,000,000 meters
Sun to Saturn distance	1,000,000,000,000 meters
Human life span	1,000,000,000 seconds
Diameter of a pencil	0.001 meter
Diameter of a bacteria	0.000001 meter

Science Numbers: From Zero to Infinity

Name _____

The Size of Things in Meters

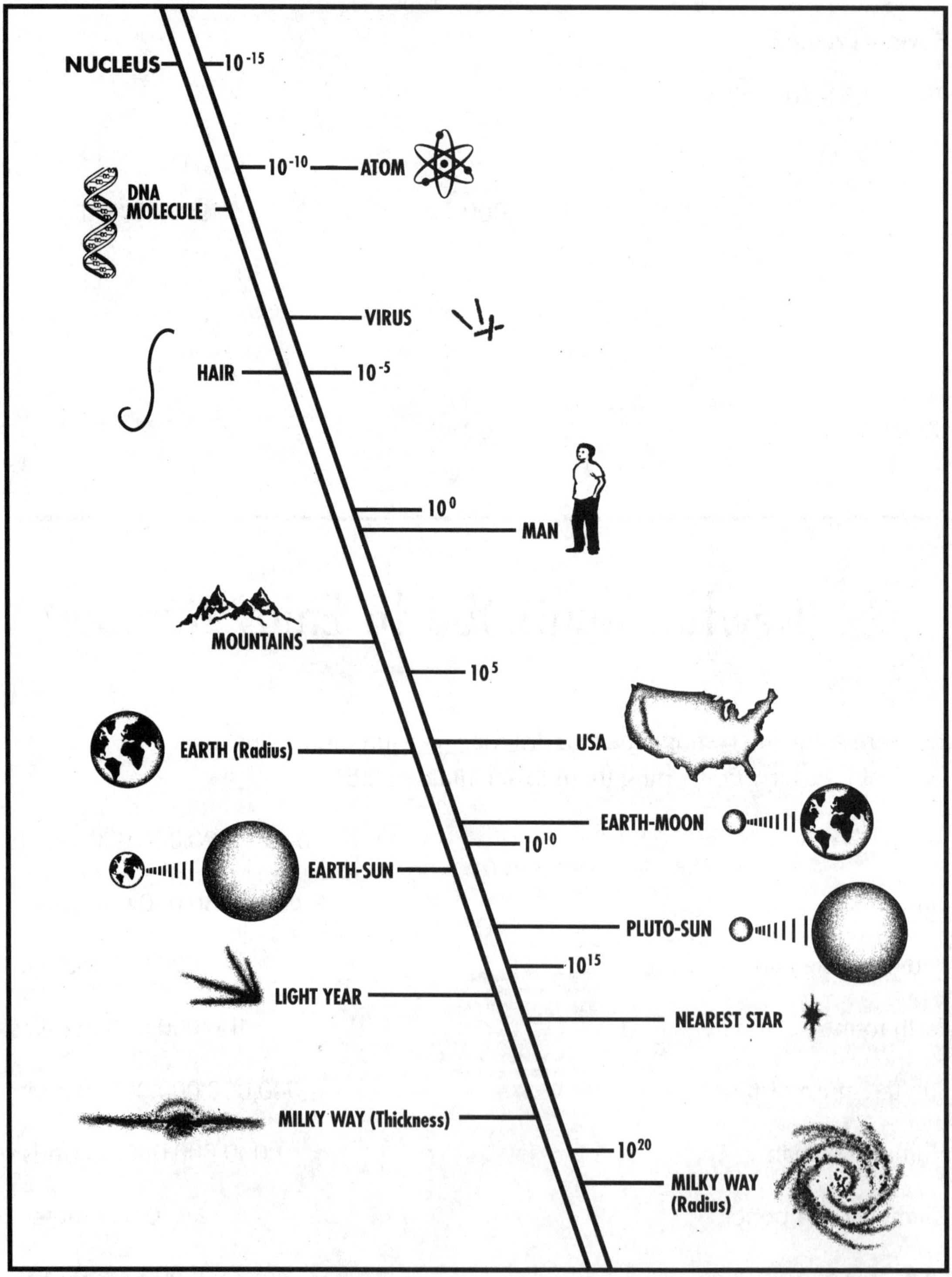

- NUCLEUS — 10^{-15}
- DNA MOLECULE — 10^{-10} — ATOM
- VIRUS
- HAIR — 10^{-5}
- 10^0 — MAN
- MOUNTAINS — 10^5 — USA
- EARTH (Radius) — EARTH-MOON
- EARTH-SUN — 10^{10}
- PLUTO-SUN
- LIGHT YEAR — 10^{15} — NEAREST STAR
- MILKY WAY (Thickness) — 10^{20} — MILKY WAY (Radius)

Name _____

Metricopter

NEWTON'S ACTION LAB
Science Fun
17

 ## Newton Wants You to Know

Pisa, Italy, is where the famous scientist Galileo worked. Near Pisa, there is a small town called Spagheterini. Outside the town of Spagheterini there is a forest fire that has been burning for many months.

The local scientists have finally developed a "bomb" that will fight forest fires. But they have a **problem**. The fire-fighting bomb is only 2.5 centimeters long and weighs only 3.7 grams. When dropped over the Spagheterini fires, they are always blown off course.

Leonardo da Vinci's helicopter model

A Spagheterinian teenager named Dominick has come up with the solution. Drop the tiny bombs hanging from tiny helicopters. To make them stable, Dominick remembered that the Chinese made helicopter toys hundreds of years ago. Leonardo da Vinci drew model helicopters around the year 1500. Helicopter rotors act like the wings of an airplane. By changing the angle of its rotor blade, a helicopter can rise straight up, hover in space or move in any direction.

Help Dominick save Spagheterini. Build some tiny helicopters. There is one problem. His helicopter design is in metric units. That is why he calls it his **metricopter**. Study the box below for help in reading metric centimeters.

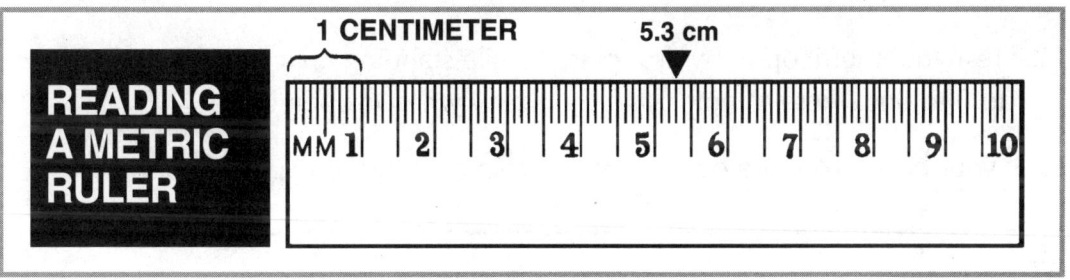

 ## Constructing Your Metricopter

1. Study the metricopter design on page 44.

2. Notice that the design is in metric units.

TLC10140 Copyright © Teaching & Learning Company, Carthage, IL 62321-0010

Metricopter

Name _____

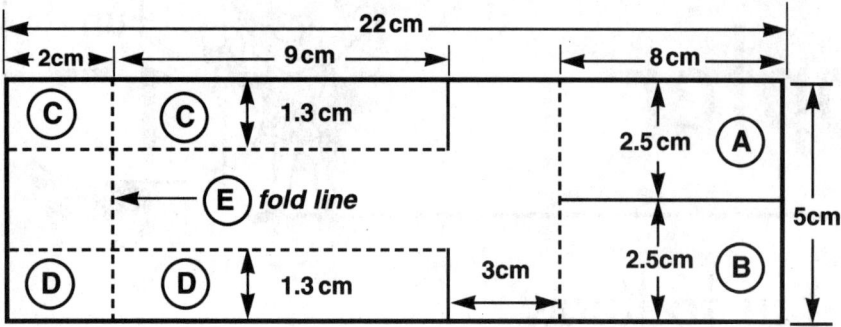

3. Construct your metricopter full size according to the metric dimensions shown on the drawing. *Do not try to cut out a metricopter the exact size of the drawing.* Do not try to trace the design on the left. It is too small. Follow the instructions below.

4. Use notebook or other paper to cut out a rectangle 22 centimeters long and 5 centimeters wide.

5. Mark off your rectangle with the dimensions shown on the drawing above.

6. Cut along all **solid** lines shown in the drawing.

7. Fold section A forward (towards you) and section B backward (away from you).

8. Fold section C in toward section D. Section C goes all the way to the bottom.

9. Fold section D in toward section C. It will overlap section C.

10. After folding C and D, fold up at line E. The fold should be a 90° right angle.

11. Compare your finished product to the sketch on the right.

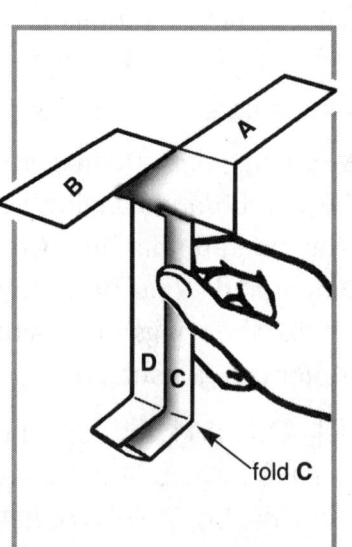

12. Test your metricopter by dropping it while standing on a chair. See the sketch to find out where to hold the metricopter when dropping.

Pack your bags. Your are on your way to join Dominick in Spagheterini.

Newton Thinks You Can Build a Better Metricopter

Your metricopter works, but it could be improved. Newton would like you to improve the design. Try different kinds of paper or cardboard. Try bigger or more wings. Try a small weight such as a paper clip on the base. Don't sit there. Try something different.

44

TLC10140 Copyright © Teaching & Learning Company, Carthage, IL 62321-0010

Name _____

Can You Measure Me?

Newton Wants You to Know

Newton measured everything around him. His famous laws are based upon repetitive and accurate measurements. He learned, as you will in this activity, that measurements must often be made indirectly.

Measuring with a Quarter

Forget inches. Forget centimeters. Why not use quarters as a unit of distance and weight?

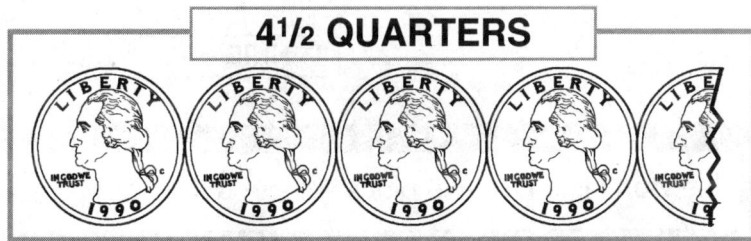

4½ QUARTERS

1. How many quarters fit across this page? _____. You can use ½ quarters and even ¼ quarters in your measuring.

2. How many quarters are in the length of this page? _____

3. How many quarters are there from your wrist to the end of your middle finger? _____

 = 5 grams

A quarter weighs about five grams. Could you use that knowledge to **estimate** how many grams are in each of the following:

4. Grams in a penny. _____

5. Grams in a half dollar. _____

6. Grams in your pen or pencil. _____

45

Can You Measure Me?

Name _____

Measuring Indirectly

1. How thick is **one** sheet of paper in this book?

Newton Hint: Measure the book thickness (ignore the covers), and divide by the number of pages. Careful! Pages are sometimes numbered on both sides.

2. What is the diameter of a tennis ball? _____

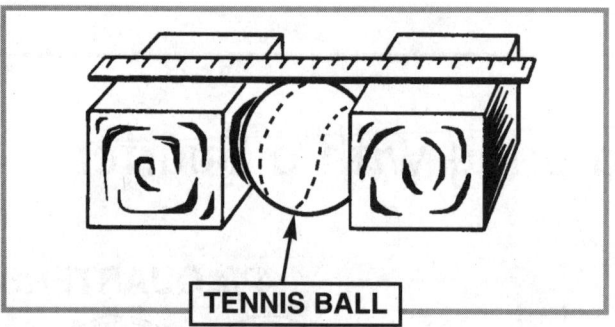

Newton Hint: Use two blocks of wood as shown.

3. What is the diameter of a copper wire? _____

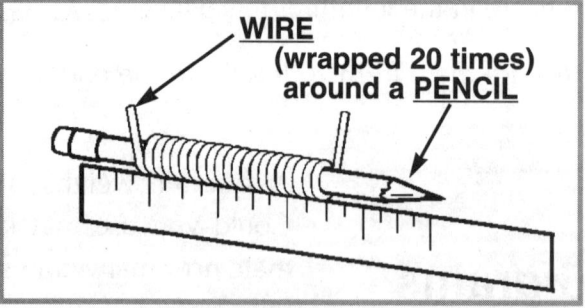

Newton Hint: You can be much more accurate if you *tightly* wrap 20 turns of wire on a pencil. Measure the total width and divide by 20. See the diagram for help.

46

TLC10140 Copyright © Teaching & Learning Company, Carthage, IL 62321-0010

Can You Measure Me?

Name _____

Weighing Newton's Famous Apple

MEASURING DEVICE

1. How much does an apple weigh? You could find out if you had a scale. You could also find out by using a kitchen volume measuring device.

   Fill the device half full of water. Add water till you get the water exactly even with one of the ounce lines. Float the apple in the water. According to Archimedes' Buoyancy Law, the apple displaces its own weight in water. If the water rises 10 ounces, your apple weighs as much as 10 ounces of water weighs. Your apple's weight in terms of displaced water is _____ ounces.

2. What is your apple's volume? This should be easy since a submerged apple displaces its own volume of water. Force the poor apple just below the surface with your finger. Note the change in volume. Your apple's volume is _____ ounces.

Newton's Measurement Challenge

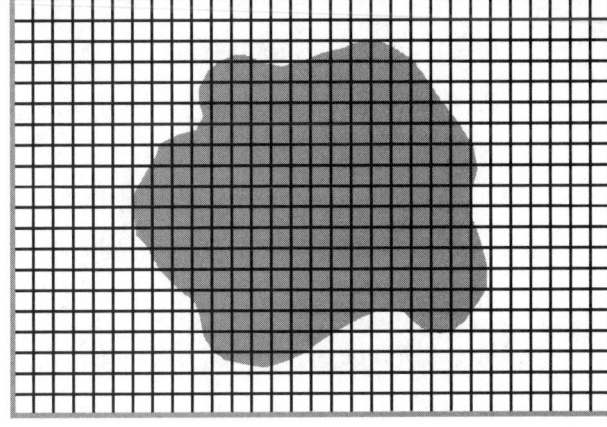

Draw an irregular shape on a piece of notebook paper. Cut it out. Can you estimate its area by using a sheet of graph paper?

A Solar Crossword Puzzle

Newton Introduction

You probably know a lot about our sun and its family in space. Here's a crossword puzzle to check your solar knowledge. You may have to do some research.

The Sun and Its Family

Across

3. The sun is a medium one
4. Largest known planetoid
8. When the moon hides the sun
9. "A chunk of iron from outer space hits the Earth in a certain place"
13. State containing the largest meteor crater
14. The planet nearly the same size as the Earth
16. Mysterious halo of light seen around the sun during an eclipse
18. Farthest planet from the Earth
20. Building blocks of which everything in the universe is made
22. Closest star to the Earth
23. Man who worked out the orbit of Halley's Comet in 1682
24. Path a revolving object takes around another object in space
28. Planet discovered in 1846
31. Another name for a *planetoid*
32. Instrument used to analyze elements on sun
34. Big head, gaseous tail, orbits the sun
35. An object spinning on its axis
37. Another name for a *meteor*
39. Familiar group or pattern of stars
40. Most familiar mark on Jupiter

Down

1. Another word for *asteroids*
2. A planetoid 18 miles (29 km) in diameter
5. A storm on the sun
6. Shooting star
7. Nine of these revolve around the sun
9. Closest planet to the sun
10. A hole in the Earth or moon showing where a meteorite hit
11. Name for the sun and all its planets
12. What we see on Mars part of the year
13. A type of lava
15. Second largest planet; has rings

48

TLC10140 Copyright © Teaching & Learning Company, Carthage, IL 62321-0010

A Solar Crossword Puzzle

Name _____

17. Eruption of gas shooting up from the surface of the sun
19. Planet discovered by Herschel in 1781
21. Force of attraction or pulling between objects in space
25. Different shapes of moon or planets as seen at different times
26. The orbiting of an object around another object in space
27. The red planet
29. 3.14
30. Our favorite planet
33. Satellites of planets
36. Layer of air or other gases around some planets
38. Greek name for the planet Mercury

THE SUN AND ITS FAMILY

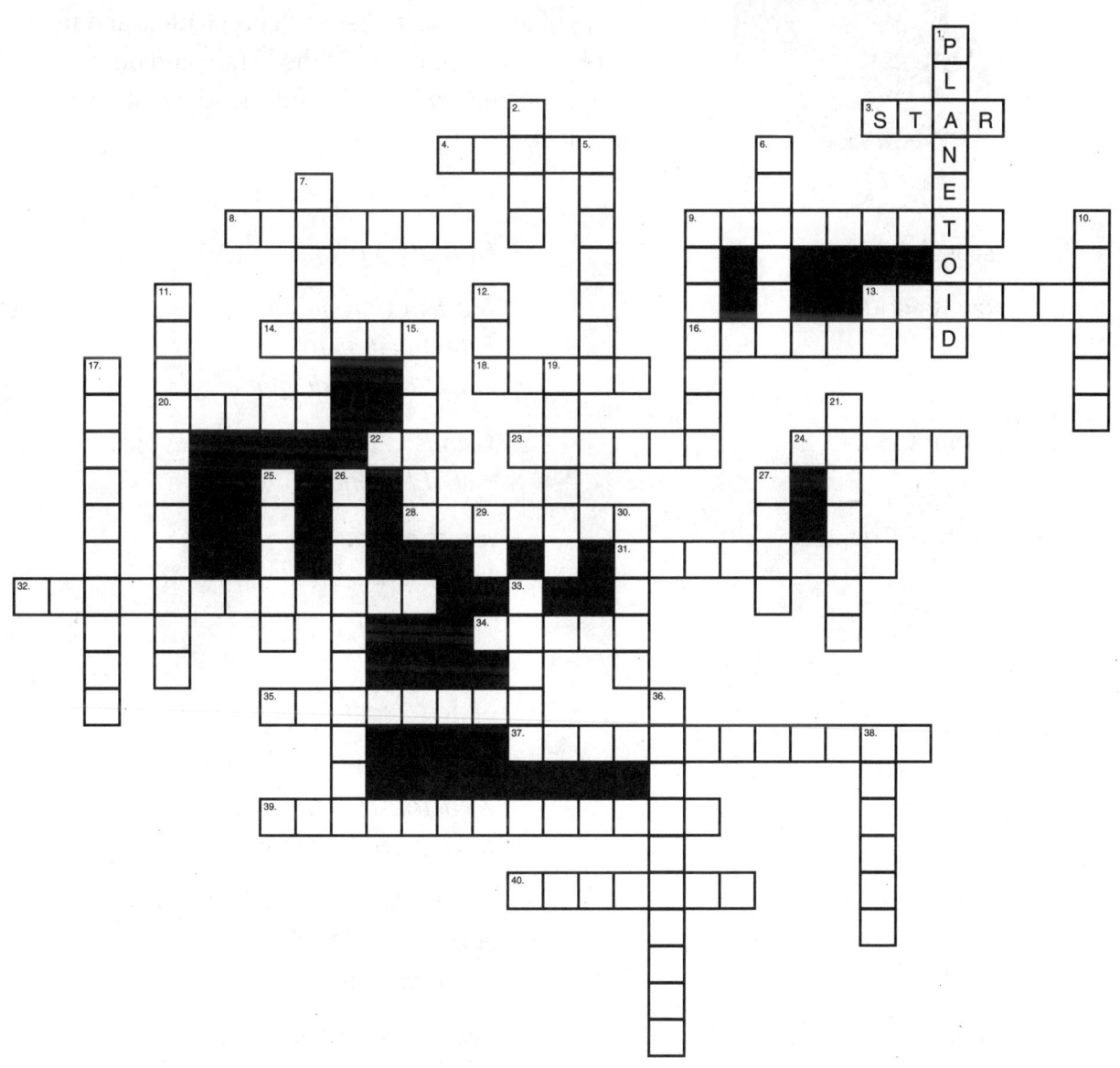

Name _____

Science Fiction

Great Science Fiction Authors

Some people make great scientific discoveries. Some scientists develop and test new products. Some people combine science and writing skills to produce great science fiction stories. Here are some of the greatest science fiction writers and their books. Find their books in the library and be thrilled and educated by their skillful blending of science and fiction.

Isaac Asimov: *Fantastic Voyage*

Ray Bradbury: *Martian Chronicles*
Fahrenheit 451
Long After Midnight

Arthur Clarke: *Islands in the Sky*
Fall of Moondust

Michael Crighton: *Jurassic Park*
Lost World

Robert Heinlein: *Farmer in the Sky*
Red Planet
Space Cadet

Andre Norton: *Star Gate*
X Factor
Judgement on Janus

Jules Verne: *20,000 Leagues Under the Sea*
Around the World in Eighty Days
Mysterious Island

H.G. Wells: *War of the Worlds*
Invisible Man

Science Fiction

Name _____

Finish This Science Fiction Story

Staci Vernebury is a normal 12-year-old in most ways. She is very athletic and loves soccer and baseball. She has brothers and sisters that she enjoys being with and sometimes, fighting with. Staci plays clarinet in the school band. She and her friends enjoy games or just talking.

There is one thing special about Staci. Her dad is a space engineer working for NASA. Her mother works for the DuPont corporation as a chemist. Her parents are extremely bright.

The day Staci was born, there was a lightning storm that knocked out the electricity in the hospital. When the electricity came back on in the delivery room, there was an unexpected surge in all the electronic devices.

At that instant, infant Staci's brain absorbed all the knowledge in her parents' heads. She suddenly knew all about space and chemistry.

As Staci grew up, she had many adventures because of her superior knowledge and mental ability. There was one day when . . .

Try to finish this story in a few paragraphs.

_____
_____
_____
_____
_____
_____
_____
_____
_____

Science Fiction

Name _____

Science Fiction on Your Own

Try to write a short **science fiction** story on your own. Look for ideas in the world around you. Invent a new object, creature or animal with special characteristics. Your story can take place on Earth, in space, in the center of the Earth or under an ocean. Your story can take place now, in the past or in the future. Place no limits on your imagination. Share your story with your friends or classmates.

_____

_____

_____

_____

_____

_____

_____

_____

_____

_____

_____

_____

_____

Name _____

Build a Better Boomerang

Newton's ACTION LAB
Science Fun
21

Newton Explains Boomerangs

Most people know that the primitive tribesmen of Australia use boomerangs. They are used to fight an enemy or to hunt game.

The most remarkable thing about the boomerang is its ability to return to the thrower if it misses the target. This can be explained by two scientific principles. The boomerang is always sent flying with a spinning motion. This spinning gives it **inertia** (resistance to change) and keeps it steady in flight. Secondly, the boomerang is slanted upward in flight. The air striking this slanted surface causes it to swing upward in a circle and return to the thrower.

Enough science principles. Here's your team's chance to build a better boomerang. Try to be as **creative** as you can. Below are the rules.

Constructing the Standard Boomerang

1. The standard boomerang must be made to the dimensions shown in the diagram.

2. The standard boomerang must be made of manila file folder cardboard.

3. Place your name on your boomerang.

Note: All arms are 4" (10 cm) from center. All arms are 3/4" (1.9 cm) wide.

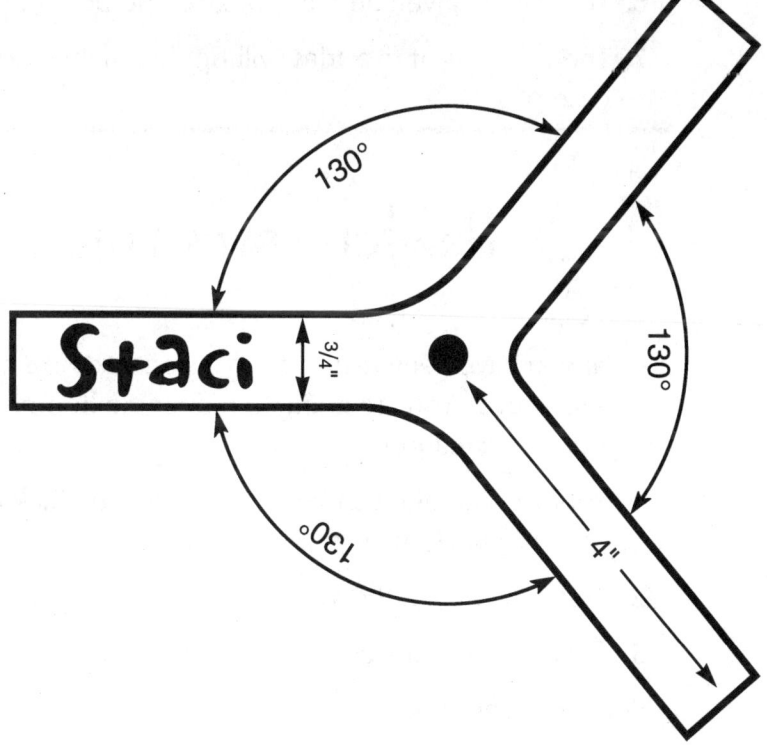

53

TLC10140 Copyright © Teaching & Learning Company, Carthage, IL 62321-0010

Build a Better Boomerang

Name _____

Launching Your Boomerang

All boomerangs will be launched from a book. Notebooks work fine.

1. Place your boomerang on the book. **Tilt the book upward**. One end of the boomerang should extend to the side of the book.
2. Strike the extended edge sharply with a ruler or pencil.

Here are the boomerang contest rules. To win, you must have the most boomerangs end up in the landing area.

1. Your boomerang must go at least 5' (1.5 m) away from the starting line.
2. Your boomerang must come back to the landing area.
3. Your launch is a success if **any part** of the boomerang extends into the landing area.

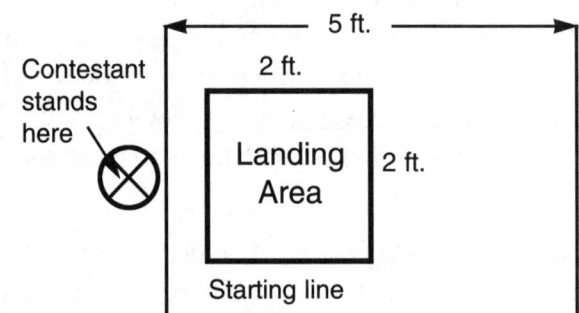

4. You will have five tries after the practice time.
5. Adjust your book angle and striking force to get into the landing zone.
6. You will be given time to practice and perfect your boomerang technique.
7. The best out of five tries will be the winner. There will be a run off contest in case of a tie.

Newton Loves Creativity

So far you have been restricted to a standard boomerang. Newton wants you to be more creative. You are going to repeat the boomerang contest using a boomerang of your own creation.

1. Your boomerang can be any size, shape, thickness or material. If you have any doubts, check with your teacher.
2. You can change the size, shape or number of wings.
3. Special bonus for being the most creative, even if you lose the contest.

Newton wishes you **good luck!**

Name _____

Paper Airplanes

Newton Wants You to Know

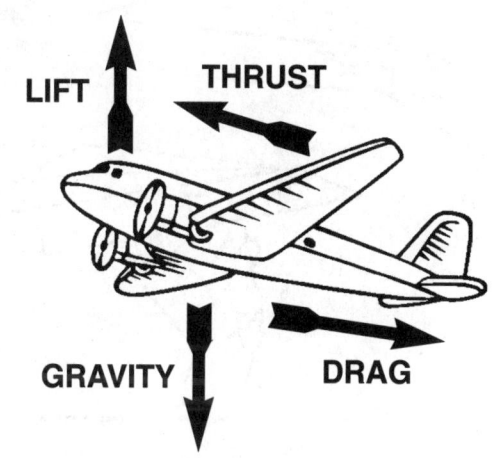

Aerodynamics is a branch of physics that studies the flow of air around and against objects. Airplane designers must follow the laws of aerodynamics or their planes won't get off the ground.

There are four forces involved in flying an airplane. They are shown at the right. **Gravity** pulls the airplane down while **lift** works against gravity to push it up. **Thrust** pushes the plane forward, while **drag** tends to slow it down.

If a plane is to fly, the positive forces of **lift** and **thrust** must exceed the negative forces of **gravity** and **drag**. The engine provides the **thrust** while the shape of the wings provides the **lift**.

This science background may help you design a better paper airplane.

Build a Simple Paper Airplane

1. Use standard notebook paper.

2. Fold it in half the long way. Press your fingers up and down the fold to leave a sharp crease.

3. Fold back one of the top corners until it meets the center.

4. Fold back the other corner the **opposite** way until it meets the center.

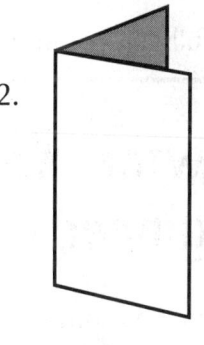

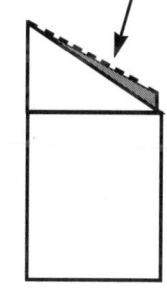

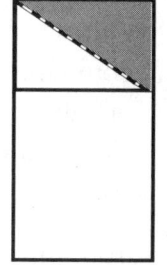

55

Paper Airplanes

Name _____

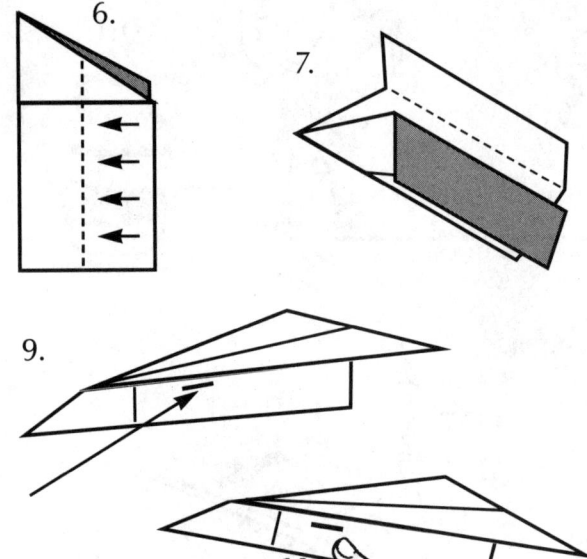

5. Use your fingers to crease both folds.

6. Fold one of your halves completely back to the center and crease. **Notice:** Not just the corner but the entire half is to be folded back.

7. Fold the other half back to the center and crease.

8. Lift the wings up so they are level with each other and at a right angle to the body. Recrease the bottom of your airplane.

9. Place a staple as shown.

10. Hold the plane between two fingers at the staple. Place the airplane above your head.

   Angle it **upward** and launch your plane. You may need to practice the launch before you get it right.

Airplane Competition

Invite others to build this simple standard paper airplane. Try having contests to achieve any of the goals listed below:

1. Furthest Flight
2. Closest to a Designated Target
3. Longest Time Afloat
4. Most Beautifully Decorated

Newton Wants You to Engineer a Better Airplane

Our simple airplane has some obvious problems. Could a better one be built? You could make it smaller or larger. Use different kinds of paper, thin cardboard, plastic or light wood. Make the wings bigger or more tilted. Could another staple or paper clip balance the plane better?

You are a future airplane designer. Build a better plane, and wait for a phone call from the Boeing Airplane Company.

Name _____

Mirror Mirage

Newton Wants You to Know

Light has been a mystery for many years. Ancient Greek philosophers thought that light came out of the eye and bounced off objects. We now know that light originates somewhere, bounces off objects and into our eye.

A mirror is a polished surface that reflects light. How many times during the day do you look into a mirror? If you stop to think about it, you probably admire your beauty at least 20 times a day. Did you ever stop to think about poor overworked light rays? They have to repeatedly make the trip to your face, bounce to the mirror and reflect into your eyes. Light rays travel at the speed of 186,000 miles (299,460 km) per second.

Mirror on Your Eyes

Draw Your Eye

Work in very bright light. Take a good look at your eye with a mirror. Can you find the opening called the **pupil** and the colored area called the **iris**? Try to make a simple sketch of your eye.

Mirror Distances

Hold a mirror 6" (15 cm) in front of your eyes. Now hold the mirror at arm's length in front of your eyes. The face you see in the mirror appears as far **behind** the mirror as your face is in **front**.

Mirror Reversal

Wink at yourself in the mirror using your right eye. Which eye appears to be blinking in your reflected image?

Smile at yourself in the mirror. Is your smiling image upside down?

57

TLC10140 Copyright © Teaching & Learning Company, Carthage, IL 62321-0010

Mirror Mirage

Name _____

Mirror Mystery

Doubling Your Money

Place a coin on a table. Hold two mirrors upright at a right angle behind the coin. Observe the coin at table level. Rotate the mirrors inward and watch your money grow.

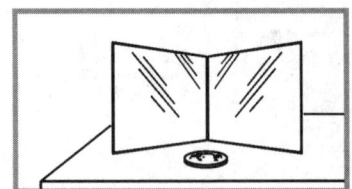

Mirror Words

Place a mirror on the dotted lines through the word *book*. Observe at eye level. You still see the word *book* because B, O and K are mirror letters. This means that the bottom of the letter mirrors the top.

There are 26 letters in our alphabet. Only nine are mirror letters. You already know about **B, O** and **K**. Can you discover the other six?

Let's assume you have discovered all nine mirror letters. Can you make up some mirror words?

Mirror Challenge

Look at a clock's face reflected in a mirror. Could you draw the clock face as you see it in the mirror? Could you use a mirror to reflect your clock drawing so that the numbers look normal? Good luck!

Making Your Own Periscope

A periscope is made of two flat mirrors. Try to position your mirrors to do the following:

1. Observe the back of your head.

2. Look at someone behind you.

3. Spy on a friend from around a corner.

A good periscope has the two mirrors in a box that keep out unwanted light rays. Tape two milk cartons together. Insert two mirrors at the same angle. Cut an opening for your eye and for the top mirror. **Go spy!**

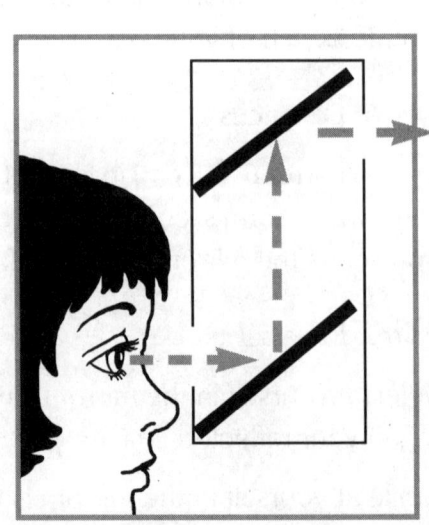

Name _____

Charged Up with Static Electricity

Newton Wants You to Know

You have already experienced static electricity. Sliding across a car seat can give you a static shock. Clothes out of the dryer tend to cling due to static electricity.

Static electricity experiments work best on dry days. On moist days, static electricity escapes into the air.

Here are some basic static electricity rules.

1. Static electricity is always due to rubbing or friction.
2. Only electrons move in static electricity experiments.
3. Static electricity is only found in nonconductors such as plastic, glass or rubber.
4. Normal objects are electrically neutral. To charge them, you must add or subtract electrons.

Simple Static Experiments

Hearing Static

Rub a large comb **vigorously** with a cloth. Wool or fur works even better. Slowly bring the comb to your ear.

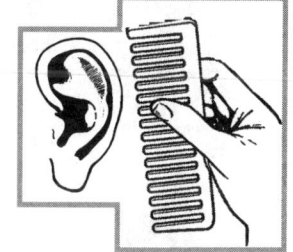

Static Pickup

Rub your comb vigorously and try to pick up various materials. Try small bits of paper and aluminum foil. Try salt and pepper. Try various cereals. Try "?".

59

Charged Up with Static Electricity

Name _____

Stubborn Paper

Tear a piece of notebook paper in half the long way. Put one half on top of the other on a table and rub vigorously with a pencil or pen.

What happened when you tried to separate the papers?

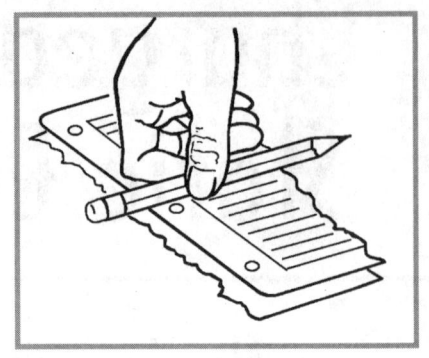

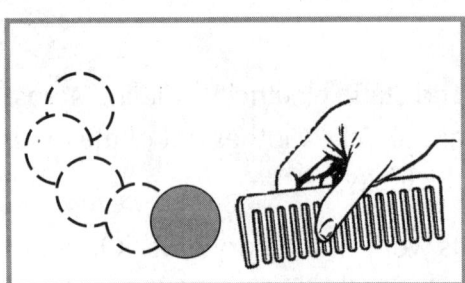

Ping-Pong™ Ball Attraction

Charge up a comb. Bring it slowly near a Ping-Pong™ ball resting on a table. It will follow you home.

Balloon Static

Charged Up Balloon

Blow up a balloon and tie a piece of light thread to it. Rub it vigorously. Hold it by the string and bring your other hand toward the balloon.

Prepare two balloons on strings. Rub them vigorously. Try to bring them together.

Hold a charged balloon near a person with dry (not oily) hair and see what happens.

Rub a balloon vigorously and attach it to a wall.

Charged Up with Static Electricity

Name _____

Static Water Stream

Keep your balloon dry during this experiment. Wet balloons do not hold static electricity.

Adjust a faucet so that you obtain a **slow** trickle of water. Charge a balloon by rubbing it. Bring it close to, but not touching, the water stream.

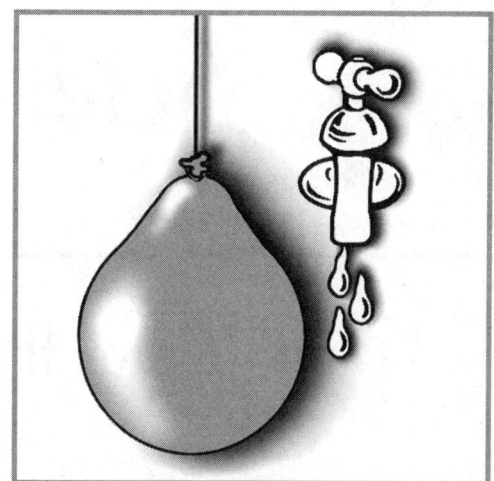

Newton Wants You to Know About Lightning

Lightning is nature's giant static electricity. A lightning stroke lights up the sky and can be heard over 20 miles (32 km) away. Your electricity at home is a little over 100 volts. Lightning can generate over 100 million volts.

Lightning usually hits the highest point in an area. The Empire State Building in New York City is hit often. You are safe in a steel building and even in a metal car. You are at risk under trees, in swimming pools or on high places such as hills or the roofs of tall buildings.

Lightning isn't all bad. The many lightning storms on Earth change the nitrogen in the air into nitrates. The nitrates fall on the Earth and provide plants with a useful fertilizer.

Science Fables

The Tale of the Foolish King

Once upon a time there lived a foolish king who thought he was very wise. He called in the people of his palace one day to prove how smart he really was. He told them he had made a wondrous scientific discovery about insects.

He set a fly on the palm of his hand. In his loudest voice he commanded the insect to fly. The fly obediently took off, flew around the room and landed back on the king's hand. Next, the king pulled off the poor insect's legs and again commanded it to fly. Off the fly went, around the room and back to the king. Now the king ripped off the poor fly's wings. Again the loud command to fly. The poor insect struggled and quivered but couldn't get off the king's hand.

The king turned triumphantly to the crowd and proclaimed his great discovery. Insects cannot fly without wings because they need wings to **hear** his commands.

How the Sea Became Salty

There once was a very rich merchant. He sailed from England to China in search of the world's wonders.

He found and bought a magic box in China. When rubbed in a circular motion, the magic box poured out salt. The merchant was thrilled with his magic box and set sail for England to become even more wealthy.

Science Fables

Name _____

On the way home, the merchant demonstrated his magic salt box for the ship's captain. He rubbed the box in a circular motion. Salt poured out of the box. It began to fill up the entire ship's deck. The merchant tried in vain to stop the box from making salt. The box would not stop. To keep the ship from going down with all this salt, the captain threw the box overboard. Even in the sea, the box continued to pour out salt.

And that is why the sea is salty.

Science Fables

The king and fly story is a make-believe fable, and so was the salt box story. Fables tell their story in an imaginative way.

Here's your challenge. Can you use your imagination to make up a fable with a **science** twist. Could your fable explain why winds blow, how the sun rises or why gravity pulls you down?

Share your fable with your class on _____.

Answer Key

Body Words, page 17

1. Villi
2. Plasma
3. Atrium
4. Rectum
5. Pylorus
6. Esophagus
7. Vein
8. Cartilage

Frog in the Well Problem, page 35

26 days

Mixed-Up Socks Problem, page 35

three socks

House and Lot Problem, page 36

lot costs $5000

Poison Pill Problem, page 36

Weigh six on each side. Weigh the heavier six using three on each side. Weigh **two** of the heavier three with one on each side.

Scientific Notation, page 41

1. 3.7×10^3
2. 2.5×10^4
3. 4×10^5
4. 2.8×10^6
5. 2×10^{-1}
6. 5×10^{-3}
7. 1.8×10^{-3}
8. 7×10^{-5}

A Solar Crossword Puzzle, page 49

Across

3. Star
4. Ceres
8. Eclipse
9. Meteorite
13. Arizona
14. Venus
16. Corona
18. Pluto
20. Atoms
22. Sun
23. Halley
24. Orbit
28. Neptune
31. Asteroid
32. Spectroscope
34. Comet
35. Rotation
37. Shooting star
39. Constellation
40. Red spot

Down

1. Planetoid
2. Eros
5. Sunspot
6. Meteor
7. Planets
9. Mercury
10. Crater
11. Solar system
12. Cap
13. AA
15. Saturn
17. Prominence
19. Uranus
21. Gravity
25. Phase
26. Revolution
27. Mars
29. Pi
30. Earth
33. Moons
36. Atmosphere
38. Apollo